T0128312

# SOCIALISM
## AND
# CAPITALISM
## THROUGH THE EYES
## OF A SOVIET ÉMIGRÉ

*Svetlana Kunin*

SOCIALISM AND CAPITALISM THROUGH
THE EYES OF A SOVIET ÉMIGRÉ

iUniverse books may be ordered through booksellers or by contacting:

iUniverse
1663 Liberty Drive
Bloomington, IN 47403
www.iuniverse.com
844-349-9409

Because of the dynamic nature of the Internet, any web addresses or links contained in this book may have changed since publication and may no longer be valid. The views expressed in this work are solely those of the author and do not necessarily reflect the views of the publisher, and the publisher hereby disclaims any responsibility for them.

Any people depicted in stock imagery provided by Getty Images are models, and such images are being used for illustrative purposes only. Certain stock imagery © Getty Images.

ISBN: 978-1-6632-0094-5 (sc)
ISBN: 978-1-6632-0679-4 (hc)
ISBN: 978-1-6632-0093-8 (e)

Library of Congress Control Number: 2020914762

Print information available on the last page.

iUniverse rev. date: 09/09/2020

"Therefore, I come to the indisputable conclusion that we must precisely now … put down all resistance with such brutality that they will not forget it for several decades." (Vladimir Lenin, leader of the first Communist government in Russia, March 1922)

"Out of gifted and sovereign people, the regime made us little screws in a monstrously big, rattling and stinking machine." (Vaclav Havel, a dissident playwright, Czechoslovakia, December 1989)

# Contents

# Preface

## Changing Trajectory of Life

My husband and I are Soviet baby boomers; we were both born in 1949. From our early childhood *Moral Code of the Builder of Communism* demanded from us to be modest, obedient, and loyal. So this is what we were—humble, honest, and naive believers in triumph of good over the bad. We also learned about awfulness of the capitalist system: exploitation, discrimination, racism, and imperialism. We learned that in the capitalist society, "person to person is a wolf," as opposite to the socialist system where "person to person is a friend." As we matured in our motherland, we discerned that we, two schlimazels, were doomed by limitations assigned to us by central planners, incapable of bribing any one to obtain necessities and no connections to important people who could help. This was a life of gradual degradation of confidence, self-respect, and any hope for a better future. Emigration was the only opportunity we had to change our life trajectory.

On July 2, 1980, we and our eight-year-old son landed at JFK. Sponsored by the Jewish Community of Baltimore, we were to spent the night at a hotel and fly to our destination the next day. When we stepped out of our plane, extreme heat met us outside, but it was nice and comfortable in the hotel room we were transferred to. There, I jumped out of the bathroom with my eyes wide open after I flushed the toilet. "Grisha!"—my husband's nickname, Russian-style—"The toilet is clogged!" After we carefully inspected it, we realized the clear water coming from the bottom of the toilet after flushing was actually a great sanitary idea. What other unfamiliar discoveries were ahead? We had no clue, but we knew very well what we left behind.

## Constructing the Socialist Order in the Soviet Union

### *Lenin*

The Union of Soviet Socialist Republics (USSR) was created as the result of the Russian Revolution of 1917 that overthrew tsarist autocracy. Vladimir Lenin, leader of the Russian Socialist Revolution, was inspired by the anticapitalistic class warfare theory of Karl Marx and Friedrich Engels, and he further developed it. After gaining power and establishing a coalition government, Lenin declared: "We shall now proceed to construct the Socialist order." Socialism ("From each according to his ability, to each according to his contribution.") is a transitional phase toward the Communism ("From each according to his ability, to each according to his needs.").

Euphoric expectations of the new era drove many Russian intellectuals to the side of the revolution. Talented poets, writers, and artists glorified the destruction of the old order and the march toward the bright future of Communism. Their paintings, posters, poems, and writings were part of the massive Soviet propaganda machine. Most of them did not anticipate the consequences of the Socialist transformation. In 1918 the Russian poet Alexander Blok, born in 1880 into a sophisticated and intellectual family, wrote the poems "Twelve" and "The Scythians" glorifying revolution. In the poem "The Twelve," Blok described twelve Bolshevik soldiers (likened to the twelve apostles of Christianity) marching through the snowy streets of Petrograd:

| | |
|---|---|
| Гуляет ветер, порхает снег. | The wind is blowing, and snow glides. |
| Идут двенадцать человек. | Twelve men are walking in crispy strides. |
| Винтовок черные ремни, | The rifles with the blackened straps, |
| Кругом - огни, огни, огни … | And all around are sparks, sparks, |
| В зубах—цигарка, примят картуз, | sparks … |
| На спину б надо бубновый туз! | Hand-rolled cigarette, and flatten cap, |
| Свобода, Свобода, | All that is missing—the Ace of Diamonds |
| Эх, Эх, без креста! | on the back! |
| | Freedom, Freedom, |
| | Yeah, Yeah, without cross! |

Excerpt from poem "The Twelve," part 2. Alexander Blok, 1918, translated by the author.

In the same year, he wrote an essay, "Intelligentsia and Revolution," in support of new revolutionary government. Two years later, disillusioned, he complained to his friends that he lost "faith in the wisdom of humanity" and that "all sounds have stopped." In February 1921, at the Pushkin Festival, Blok pleaded for the "freedom of creation." His mental and physical health had deteriorated. Lenin's government didn't allow him to leave for medical treatment abroad. He died in August 1921.

## War Communism

In 1918 under the banner of "Factories to workers, Land to peasants, Power to people!" policies of militant Communism (war Communism, Военный коммунизм) were implemented. A Decree on Land transferred ownership of property to the government; a Decree on Government Monopoly on banks included confiscation of savings, gold, and silver. A new Soviet government nationalized factories, railroads, and media.

By 1921, the Soviet population had come face-to-face with the disastrous consequences of militant Communism. The government's monopoly on the production and distribution of agricultural products led to severe famine that killed millions. To fight hunger, other countries were asked for help. Looking for additional sources of income, Lenin issued a decree authorizing the confiscation of all valuable assets from religious institutions. On March 19, 1922, he wrote a letter to members of the Politburo (Executive Committee of the Communist Party) marked, "Please make no copies for any reason." The letter said:

Наоборот, для нас именно в данный момент представляет из себя не только исключительно благоприятный, но и вообще единственный момент, когда мы можем 99-ю из 100 шансов на полный успех разбить неприятеля на голову и обеспечить за собой необходимые для нас позиции на много десятилетий. Именно теперь и только теперь, когда в голодных местностях едят людей и на дорогах валяются сотни, если не тысячи трупов, мы можем (и поэтому должны) провести изъятие церков¬ных ценностей с самой бешеной и беспощадной энергией и не останавливаясь перед подавлением какого угодно сопротивления. Именно теперь и только теперь громадное большинство крестьянской массы будет либо за нас, либо во всяком случае будет не в состоянии поддержать сколько-нибудь решительно ту горстку черносотенного духовенства и реакционного городского мещанства, которые могут и хотят испытать политику насильственного сопротивления советскому декрету … Поэтому я прихожу к безусловному выводу, что мы должны именно теперь дать самое решитель¬ное и беспощадное сражение черносотенному духовенству и подавить его сопротивление с такой жестокостью, чтобы они не забыли этого в течение нескольких десятилетий …

Чем большее число представителей реакционного духовенства и реакционной буржуазии удастся нам поэтому поводу разстрелять, тем лучше.

For us, on the other hand, precisely at this moment we are presented with an exceptionally favorable and unique opportunity when we can, in ninety-nine out of one hundred chances, utterly defeat our enemy with total success and guarantee for us the necessary positions for many decades to come. Now and only now, when people are being eaten in famine-stricken areas and hundreds, if not thousands, of corpses lie on the roads, we can (and therefore must) pursue the removal of church property with the most frenzied and ruthless energy and not hesitate to put down any opposition. Now and only now, the vast majority of peasant masses either will be on our side or at least will not be able to provide any substantial support to handful of Black Hundreds clergy and reactionary urban petty bourgeoisie who are willing and able to attempt to oppose Soviet decree with a policy of force …

Therefore, I come to the indisputable conclusion that we must precisely now smash the Black Hundreds clergy most decisively and ruthlessly and put down all resistance with such brutality that they will not forget it for several decades …

The greater the number of representatives of reactionary clergy and reactionary bourgeoisie we will succeed in executing, the better.

Svetlana Kunin

Antireligious propaganda demonizing and ridiculing religion accompanied this campaign. A new magazine titled *Godless* (Безбожник) popularized the image of atheists (the godless) as modern and cool. Facing the urgent necessity to infuse life into the failing economy, Lenin set forth a New Economic Policy (NEP) that replaced militant Communism. In a sense, the policy was a partial implementation of economic principles of capitalism. It allowed free enterprise, private property, and some foreign investments. In one year, the economy was back to the prewar level.

At the same time, Lenin concentrated on tighter control of the government and elimination of opposition to the dominant authority of the Bolshevik party. On his order in 1923, Solovki Special Purpose Camp (Solovetski Lager OsobogoNaznachenia, or SLON) was established on the Solovetsky Islands in the White Sea, a secluded location where a historic monastery stood and that had been used for the czar's prisons since the fifteenth century. This was the first Soviet model of forced-labor camps. Thousands of religious leaders, aristocrats, and intelligentsia who had expressed reservations about the new state of the country were accused of counterrevolutionary activities, subjected to public humiliation, denounced, and deported to SLON.

The framework for the first Socialist country was based on Karl Marx's vision of the dictatorship of the proletariat. The concept was further developed by Lenin: "The dictatorship of the proletariat is a stubborn struggle—bloody and bloodless, violent and peaceful, military and economic, educational and administrative—against the forces and traditions of the old society." (V. I. Lenin. Collected Works, XXV, 190)

The dictatorship of the proletariat was represented by the Communist Party's monopoly on power.

Lenin died in January 1924 supposedly from complications of a stroke, but scholars have since determined the cause was neurosyphilis.

*Stalin*

In 1925, following a power struggle between old revolutionary party leaders Joseph Stalin, Leon Trotsky, Lev Kamenev, and Grigory Zinoviev, Stalin consolidated power in his hands. To eliminate potential political challenges to his authority, Stalin orchestrated a series of show trials accusing his opponent of assassination plots against government officials. As a result, most of the surviving old revolutionary leaders were executed.

To finalize the transformation of the Soviet Union to a Socialist state, Stalin launched a "revolution from above." In 1928 he replaced the New Economic Policy with centrally developed and controlled Five-Year Plans. For the industrial sector, he concentrated on developing heavy industrial machinery and military equipment. On the agricultural side, he issued a decree converting individual farms into state collective farms. The *kulaks*, a million or so families of wealthier peasants who objected to collectivization, were deported to newly created forced-labor camps. These camps were managed by the Main Administration of Corrective Labor Camps (*Glavnoe Upravlenie inspravitel'no trudovykh LAGerei*, or gulag).

The focus on production of heavy machinery resulted in chronic shortages of consumer goods. And, as with militant Communism, forced collectivization of production and distribution of agricultural products led to a 1932–33 famine known as Holodomor (death from starvation) in which an estimated six million perished. The most severe consequences were in the Ukrainian Republic, where the biggest proportion of kulaks—the most productive and hard-working farmers—were persecuted.

During the 1920s, the first years of the Soviet era, all forms of art enjoyed a period of true renaissance. In the 1930s the Central Committee of the Communist Party declared its authority to direct all forms of art, including literature, theater, and music, – toward Soviet Realism. Nonconformists, often the most talented people, were denounced and expelled from the official professional unions. In the mid-1930s Stalin began the Great Purge. Public demonization of insubordinates, humiliation, torture to obtain admission of guilt, condemnation, and, finally, show trials and deportation or execution were the tools. The foot soldiers included not only secret police but neighbors, colleagues, and other snitches in the workplace.

Joining the kulaks and just ordinary people in the labor camps were artists, writers, scientists, philosophers, engineers, religious leaders, and Red Army commanders.

"Is there anywhere else," poet Osip Mandelstam wondered, "where poetry is so common a motive for murder?"

From the first Five-Year Plan starting in 1928, gulag prisoners were a source of free forced labor. The average life expectancy of a camp prisoner was one winter, according to a study of Soviet archives by the Hoover Institution.

In a November 2003 article in *Capitalist* magazine, Anne Applebaum, who spent years researching the archives, estimated that "the number of people with some experience of imprisonment in Stalin's Soviet Union could have run as high as 25 million, about 15 percent of the population."

The Great Purge was interrupted by World War II, when in the summer of 1941, Germans invaded the USSR. Soviets were fighting for survival of the motherland. Among them were special units consisting of gulag prisoners who fought at the war fronts that were most doomed. The Germans initially made huge advances, killing hundreds of thousands of Soviet troops. They swiftly took control of a huge part of the USSR, inflicting unprecedented cruelty on civilians in the territories they occupied. During World War II, the USSR lost twenty million civilians and suffered the highest number of military losses.

During the Great Purge, Stalin had eliminated and exiled thousands of professional military officers. But now panicked, Stalin had to recall surviving military officers and addressed the whole nation, even the remnants of the Russian Orthodox Church, appealing to nationalistic patriotism.

The horror, the suffering, the fear, and the desperation of World War II left deep scars in the psyche of every Soviet citizen who survived the ordeal. One of my uncles, who turned eighteen in 1944 and was called to the war front, came back disabled. My father was severely wounded in 1943, recovered, returned to fight, and was in the Soviet Army that stormed Berlin.

Following World War II, Stalin returned to the unfinished business of clearing the population from independent thinkers. Exposure to the capitalist life was a concern; thousands of German prisoners of war and Soviet ex-prisoners returning from Germany were sent to gulags. It became clear that anti-Semitism in the USSR was not a thing of the past. Anti-Semites in the Communist Party apparatus didn't hide their attitude. In September 1948 Stalin demanded that prominent Jewish author Ilya Ehrenburg publish an article in *Pravda* (a major Communist Party newspaper) asserting that Zionism contradicts Communist ideology and that Jews in Socialist countries shouldn't have anything to do with the country of Israel. The propaganda campaign was followed by the liquidation of prominent Jewish organizations and individuals.

In 1948 the Jewish Anti-Fascist Committee members, who during World War II raised funds abroad for the Soviet Union, were accused of bourgeois nationalism and allegiance to anti-Communist ideology (cosmopolitism). They were tortured, put through show trials, and executed. Committee chairman Solomon Mikhoels, noted director of the Yiddish State Theater was murdered by the Soviet secret police in a staged car accident. In 1952 came the Doctors' Plot, when nine prominent Moscow doctors, six of them Jewish, were publicly accused of conspiracy to assassinate Soviet leaders.

Stalin's Great Purge was catastrophic for the fate of millions of unfortunate human beings and the lives of their loved ones. Those less directly affected were besieged by progovernment propaganda. Information about arrests of "enemies of the people" was accompanied with posters, movies, etc. glorifying the great leader presiding over the just and fair Socialist society, free from the greedy exploiters. Repressions and suppression of descent was accompanied by mass propaganda, glorifying ideas of Socialism on the way of bright future of Communism.

Stalin died in 1953 and was succeeded by the First Secretary of the Communist Party, Nikita Khrushchev.

## *Khrushchev - End of Stalinism*

In 1956 Khrushchev denounced Stalin's deeds and exposed his purges and executions. Lenin, however, continued to be glorified and idolized. Under Khrushchev in 1956, the Hungarian Uprising against the Soviet-imposed government was brutally suppressed; in 1961 the Berlin Wall was built to prevent people from escaping from East Germany to the West; in 1962 Soviets tried to place ballistic nuclear missiles in Cuba (Cuban Missile Crisis). Still, Khrushchev was concerned about the USSR's international image. Art was liberalized, previously prohibited books were printed, and scientists worked on the space program.

Khrushchev may have been the last Soviet leader who actually believed the USSR could achieve the Communist ideal. He was removed from power in an internal coup of the Communist Party and "voluntarily" retired in 1964.

The next General Secretary of the Communist Party of the USSR was Leonid Brezhnev. His Five-Year Plans were aimed at the buildup of the powerful military and creation of an economy to overtake the gross national product of the United States—a goal neither he nor his successors were ever able to achieve. By the 1970s, hysteria of Stalin's era, like public show trials and millions of gulag prisoners, were a thing of the past, although not totally eliminated. Covert snitches were embedded at places of work, schools, army bases, and research centers; media and art were strictly censored.

# 1

# From Villages and Shtetls to the Big Cities

My grandparents lived in a small town of Bobruisk in the republic of Belarus. Before the Russian Revolution of 1917, Bobruisk was part of the Jewish Pale of Settlement area where Jews were allowed to live in tsarist Russia. My maternal grandfather (1898–1950) was a builder who remodeled old houses and built new ones. He built a three-room house where he and our grandmother lived and raised their five children. In a little plot of land adjacent to the house, my grandmother grew vegetables—enough for the family to eat and sell at the local bazaar.

1949. My grandparents with their adult children: three daughters, two sons, son in-law, and grandchildren. My grandmother is holding me. Seated children are (left to right) my cousin, my brother, and my sister.

The old order was destroyed, and boundaries of the Jewish Pale of Settlement had been eliminated. Like birds released from a cage, young Jewish teenagers were rushing toward previously forbidden education and opportunities in the big cities. Among them were my mother and father. The Constitution of the USSR, which was established in 1936, guaranteed all rights and protection for the citizens of the USSR. Article 112, chapter IX declared that "judges are independent and subject only to the law," and chapter X guaranteed fundamental rights of citizens, including freedom of speech, press, assembly, and demonstrations. The country needed doctors, engineers, lawyers, and other professionals educated and molded by the new system. In 1934 my father was accepted in the law program at the University of Minsk. His graduation coincided with the beginning of World War II. In 1939 before my father left to join the army, he married Maria Karaeva, the girl from his town of Bobruisk.

By the time I was born in 1949, many people understood that their real rights were subject to the interpretation of the Secretary General of the Communist Party and Central Bureau of the Communist party in Moscow. I believe my parents' hopes of a better, brighter future helped them to adapt and forced them to conform.

# 2

## The Socialist Way of Life

Official compensation for every working person in the country was set by the government independent of skills, talents, and efforts. Such equality in compensation, in combination with chronic deficits, created a unique social hierarchy in the Soviet society. Communist apparatchiks, who controlled all areas of the economy, and military professionals had access to special stores that were closed to the public. After them, the highest status on the social ladder of respectable occupations belonged to people involved in sales, storage, and distribution of any kind of goods. Not only did they have access to the deficit supplies, but they could arrange useful exchanges with other people who were considered respectable. Next were occupations with the potential access to deficit supplies: doctors through patients, lawyers through clients, tailors though customers, and even teachers through students' parents. The least practical profession was in engineering or any other occupation that did not have access to distribution channels or useful clients.

There was a joke that rephrased the second item from the Moral Code of the Builder of Communism (1961): "He, who does not work, neither shall eat," became, "He, who does not work *here*, neither shall eat."

For the average Soviet citizen, providing for the family was not a simple task. In Minsk, the capital of Belarus Republic where we lived, as in other capital cities, whole grains, bread, potatoes, milk, and very limited assortments of meats were usually available. The best selection was in Moscow, capital of the USSR. People from the rest of the country came to the capital cities for the food supplies.

To retain some self-esteem and self-respect in the world where your talents or efforts didn't really matter, Soviet intelligentsia incorporated world cultural treasures into their lives. Emerging into the immaterial world of music, literature, art, movies, and theater helped them cope with day-to-day hardship over the basic necessities and retain some human dignity.

But for many people, the way to deal with lack of individual liberties and opportunities was to dull the senses with alcohol. This cultural trait resulted in a large percentage of alcoholics, especially men; it was a huge burden on family life and was especially hard for the women.

# 3

# Growing Up in the USSR

My parents, a lawyer and a librarian, were honest, sober, follow-the-rules Soviet citizens. They silently witnessed the return of open anti-Semitism, continued even after Stalin's death in 1953. After World War II, the official government position was that Jews educated before the war occupied too many influential positions, and now they should be replaced by a newly educated cadre of Russians. A wave of media-covered trials exposing often fabricated corruption, demotions, imprisonment, and even executions marked that period. Thankfully, our dedicated and uncompromisingly honest father survived.

We lived in a two-room apartment with a kitchen and bathroom. My sister, brother, and I shared one room, and our parents had a separate room. We were lucky; many families at that time had roommates in one apartment and a shared kitchen and bathroom. In the 1960s, modern conveniences like refrigerators, washing machines, and televisions appeared in stores. Trying to save money to buy these new appliances, our father started to teach law at Minsk University in the evenings after his day job. Still, there was not enough money for even the day-to-day expenses of food and clothing. Our parents tried to shelter us from the hardship of life. They were very much aware that wrong conversation could put the family in jeopardy, so they never discussed political events in front of us, but often we heard our parents arguing about their shortage of money.

When I was a child, my father read to me fairy tales and shared his idealism and beliefs of the triumph of good over evil. In school we were taught patriotism. I learned about the "fathers of the revolution" in nursery school by singing songs about grandpas Lenin and Stalin. To reinforce loyalty to the Socialist society, everyone from age seven to twenty-eight was enrolled in a political entity. First, at seven years old, came *Octiabrenok* where we wore a star pin with a picture of Lenin. Then there was *Pioneer* with the red scarf around the neck. Then, from age fourteen to twenty-eight, it was *Komsomoletz*, young Communists proudly displaying the pin that symbolized the flame of the revolution. Membership in the Communist Party required approvals by party leaders; it was reserved for those seeking an advanced career or position. I was a good and enthusiastic Octiabrenok, Pioneer, and Komsomoletz, oblivious to the experiences of my parents' generation except the horror of war.

We studied how capitalists exploited the proletariat in capitalist countries, especially in the United States, and how the ideals of Socialism and Communism set forth by Karl Marx and Friedrich Engels were much superior. When in 1961 the Moral Code of the Builder of Communism was developed, we were required to memorize and recite it before our class peers.

1961. Svetlana is second from the right in the first row.

# 4

# Reality Sets In

My acquaintance with reality was gradual. In 1956 Khrushchev denounced Stalin's era purges, and Stalin's name was removed from the patriotic texts, songs, and images. Khrushchev allowed some information to surface. People realized what had happened during the Stalin years. I learned, for example, that a majority of the Soviet authors I read and loved—Mikhail Bulgakov, Boris Pasternak, Yury Olesha, Mikhail Zoshchenko, Osip Mandelstam, Anna Akhmatova, Isaac Babel, and so many more—ended up physically or psychologically destroyed by government orders. Their ideology did not fit with demands of Socialist conformity.

Multitudes of scientists, artists, and musicians were expelled from their professional unions because the nature of their work was not in line with the official party line. Among them were great filmmakers such as Sergei Eisenstein and composers such as Sergei Prokofiev and Dmitri Shostakovich who were denounced for "neglect of ideology and subservience to Western influence." These discoveries came as a hard blow.

The realization that we were not of the right breed came when we enrolled to school. From birth on, a Soviet citizen's ethnicity was part of every official document: on birth certificates, passports, diplomas, and even library cards there was a line indicating our ethnicity. We were Jewish. I became familiar with some Jewish history by reading books like *Joseph and His Brothers* by Thomas Mann and *The War of the Jews* by Lion Feuchtwanger, translated to Russian.

In the 1950s the Communist Party imposed acceptance quotas

for Jewish students in institutions of higher education. The most prestigious institutions of higher learning hardly accepted any Jews. My sister dreamed of being a doctor but was rejected from medical school. The next year she passed exams to the Polytechnic Institute of the Belarus Republic, where Jews were allowed in bigger numbers. My brother went to the Engineering School in Leningrad. I wanted to be a lawyer or psychologist, but in 1967, on the realistic advice of my brother, I followed my sister's steps to the Polytechnic Institute in Minsk. To be accepted, our grades had to be competitive. On average there were ten to twelve applicants for every opening in these colleges. All courses in Soviet colleges were assigned, not selected. In addition to general and specialty courses, we studied Marxist and Leninist theories in more depth.

Svetlana (left) with childhood friend Tatiana. High school, 1966

In 1968, during summer vacation after our first year in college, my friends and I decided to travel to the northern part of our country: Karelia and then Leningrad. Our resources were very limited, so our backpacks were loaded with canned food, tents, and the like. For transportation we mostly hitchhiked or, when necessary, used public buses, trains, and ferries.

1968 summer vacation. Svetlana is second from front.

The Soviet Union had captured Karelia from Finland in 1940 in the Winter War. At that time more than four hundred thousand people fled from this territory to Finland. Only about five thousand remained under Soviet control. The people and places we visited were very different from our very Soviet city of Minsk. They all despised Soviets.

In Karelia we saw abandoned houses and beautiful old churches slowly deteriorating.

We were traveling on our own, meeting all kinds of people, and listening to their very unfamiliar stories. One truck driver who picked us up told us how his family was separated when the Soviets annexed this land from Finland. To us, his contempt for the USSR was as strange as it was obvious.

Then we took a ferry to Kizhi Island and then on to the Solovetsky Islands to see unique wooden houses and churches built without nails. On the Solovetsky Islands people also showed us an old monastery and prisons where both Russian tsars and Bolsheviks had banished the unfaithful. This was part of the SLON prison system established by Lenin and later expended and transition to gulags.

A man who lost his arms in World War II told us how in the 1960s he and others who lost limbs in the war didn't want to be a burden on their families and therefore lived on the streets of big cities, begging for food or money. Most of the people who lived through the war could not pass by without giving them something, he said. When Khrushchev opened the USSR to foreign visitors to promote an image of a vibrant and happy Soviet society, beggars were taken off the streets and deported to the Solovetskys. That brought memories from our childhoods, how disabled beggars were part of the scenery in the central area of Minsk but then suddenly disappeared. For us, the Solovetsky Islands were the first glimpse of the reality of human helplessness in the face of government power.

Another blow to my patriotic enthusiasm came in 1968 when the Soviet Army invaded Czechoslovakia to crush a democratic movement for reforms and independence. All the Socialist rhetoric about fairness and justice did not correspond to the Socialist government actions.

# 5

# The Time of Maturity

I met Grigory, my future husband, in Bobruisk. My college friend Eugenia and I chose Bobruisk Construction Company for our summer internship after our third year in college. I stayed with my grandmother in her house, and Eugenia stayed at her distant relative's house while they were on vacation. One weekend, Eugenia and I invited my two cousins for dinner at her place. We were having a good time with some wine and music when the owner's son unexpectedly walked into his parents' house. This was a shocking surprise.

Grigory had studied electrical engineering and had just completed his internship in Minsk. He came home, unaware of the guests. Luckily, he was not a prude; to the contrary, he played drums in the college band and appreciated good company. I think he was ready to marry me at first site. Grigory took my number and in a few months invited me and Eugenia to his birthday party at his parents' house. He also invited his band with all the musical instruments. I thought that the house would collapse from the sounds of the band. But it survived, as did other houses in the neighborhood. I was impressed. Our wedding took place in March 1971.

We rented a room from a couple in a two-room apartment. We were in our last year at college, both working on our final projects. Our parents helped us with the rent, and Grigory tried to find some temporary jobs to pay for food. I had to learn how to cook. At that time in the USSR people did not eat out, and there was no such thing as takeout. Moving out of our parents' homes was the beginning of real life. Until this time, our parents carried the load of providing for our needs, and all the surrounding media, movies, and teachings instilled expectations of a better life ahead.

After graduation, Grigory was assigned to work in Minsk, and I got free assignment, meaning that I had to find a job on my own. It took many days walking from door to door of multiple civil engineering companies and being rejected after seeing a record in my diploma that I was Jewish. I finally came to a company where the project leader was Azerbaijani (another republic in the Union). He was assembling group for his new technology automation project, didn't mind my Jewishness, and liked my young enthusiasm. I became a system analyst in the civil engineering construction company.

A year later I was pregnant, and our landlords asked us to leave because they didn't want any inconveniences. We moved back with my parents. Grigory changed jobs and started working as a field service engineer. This job required high qualifications and a lot of travel, so the pay was a little bit higher. There were not enough qualified people who wanted to travel; therefore, even Jews could be hired.

We were on the waiting list for a public apartment. The estimated wait was more than ten years. Another option was to pay for the apartment in the cooperative building, but there were too many people for this option also; nobody accepted our names for the waiting list. This was the Socialist process for any change: applying to the government agency for permission, waiting for a response, and then, if we were turned down, starting all over again or just giving up. After realizing that there was no hope for our own place within the foreseeable future, I made an appointment with the local Communist Party Bureau director responsible for the living accommodations in Minsk. I told him that my husband didn't get along with my mother and that my father in addition to his full-time job as a lawyer taught law in the evening at the university and needed space to prepare. The director finally replied that all my reasons meant nothing. Surprisingly, he gave me a letter authorizing the entry of our names on the waiting list for a new development. His secretary told me that it was dumb luck; he had a daughter my age and probably felt sorry for me. So this time I was lucky. Whatever the reason for his mercy, in three years we moved into our own apartment.

Soviet people dealt with life as it was presented to them. We had friends. We loved music and movies. We celebrated holidays and birthdays. But we did not have the option to see life outside the Soviet borders. Our perception of the world could come only from government-controlled sources. The majority still believed in the ideals of Socialism and Communism and in the greatness and superiority of the USSR. Some of us tried to listen to Voice of America or the BBC, but those broadcasts were often jammed. Even with the equality of income, there were still differences in the personal levels of happiness and misery. People were envious of a peer's promotions or neighbors' and friends' connections or talents. Most families struggled with low salaries, but families where one or more members were heavy drinkers struggled more. Often alcoholism was reason for divorce; but in many cases, divorcees continued to live in one apartment, unable to physically separate.

The Soviet economy suffered from chronic stagnation. Collectivized agriculture never achieved the productivity of prerevolutionary Russia. Food was always in short supply even with an established program that sent urban residents to the collective farms (*kolkhozes*) to help with seeding in spring and harvesting in fall. Twice a year, engineers, scientists, doctors, college students, professors, and factory workers spent from two to six weeks working as low-level agricultural laborers.

There were special hospitals, schools, and vacation places allocated to the party leaders and high-ranking government officials. The rest of the society dealt with unsanitary hospitals with outdated equipment, shortages, and waiting lines. Despite the almost complete elimination of any religious associations and practices, anti-Semitism in the USSR was ingrained in the government and trickled down into the day-to-day life; it determined our occupation and career advancement.

At the age of twenty-eight we had pretty much accomplished what we could in terms of career, salary, and other possible aspirations. We were boxed into structure defined for us by the central government. The only way out of the box involved corruption. Laws applied only to the masses outside the governing circle and its acolytes. The Constitution, the Moral Code of the Builder of Communism, and all the rhetoric about superiority of classless society were just a brainwashing mantra used by politburo rulers to keep symbiotic coexistence with the people they herded. Outside the circle of friends and relatives, the life of an individual human being was as relevant or irrelevant as political bureaucrats decreed. The government's power over the life and fate of any citizen was obvious and frightening.

# 6

# Breaking Out

In the early 1970s, Soviet dissidents were able to pass their stories on to foreign human rights activists, many brave Americans among them. The reality of Soviet life, the discrimination, and the suppression of dissent were exposed to the world. International pressure started to build. Facing a straggling economy, the USSR sought normalized trade status with the United States.

In exchange for the import of American grain, the Soviet government allowed Jews to immigrate. The fact that Jews were allowed to immigrate was a miracle. We applied for permission to immigrate in 1979. Our parents had to sign our papers, indicating that they did not object to our request. For my father, who for twenty years was head of the Law Department in Ministry of Auto-transportation of Belarus, this signature meant the end of his professional life.

Sad, but without hesitation, my father signed the required papers. Our Soviet citizenship was revoked. We sold everything we owned to repay the government for our education and emigration visas, and in April 1980 we left the USSR.

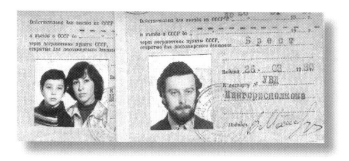

*Svetlana Kunin*

A few months later, my brother followed us with his wife and three-year-old son.

Many years later, we found out that after we left USSR, our father was publicly condemned for giving us permission to leave; his Communist Party membership was revoked, and he was forced to retire from his job.

My father was a dreamer. In his young years he was believer into righteousness of Socialism. He was also too intelligent to not eventually realize that there is no future for his children in that system.

# 7

# Freedom

### New Culture

On July 2, 1980, sponsored by the Baltimore Jewish Community, we stepped onto American soil. Unexpectedly, smiling people were ready to help. Unaccustomedly Christian churches and Jewish synagogues were plentiful and coexisted without problems. People weren't afraid or embarrassed to worship. Jews weren't embarrassed to be Jews. Music and culture were infused with a mixture of ethnicities.

After being brainwashed for thirty years about the ugly face of capitalism, it was awesome for us to see a society as dynamic and diverse as America. I admired how mercifully the disabled and sick were treated by individuals and society as a whole. Charity was a new and wondrous part of our new life. Jewish family services lent us money and provided tutoring in English until we were able to find jobs. We were issued green cards, which gave us permission to work in the United States. We were grateful for the help, but we did not expect it to last. We had to learn how to live in the competitive world of America. In order to find jobs, we needed to have a car and learn how to drive. Our first car was a 1972 Dodge Coronet that we bought for $450. We proudly posed in front of our big and beautiful vehicle, took pictures with a Polaroid camera that we'd bought at local flee market for two dollars, and sent pictures to our parents in the Soviet Union.

Going through job interviews was a new and quite unnerving experience. We had been taught that modesty is the way. Therefore, presenting ourselves in a self-promoting way wasn't easy. Humble

Grigory had a difficult time at job interviews. I was trying to bring his confidence out from the cocoon of modesty. That involved some yelling. I was better at self-promotion, but my English was abysmal. So, when a small printing company offered me the position of data entry clerk, I was quite happy. In a month Grigory found a job as an electronic technician at Martin Marietta, today's Lockheed Martin.

We were very happy! I shared my excitement with my boss and was confused when he expressed regrets that an electrical engineer had to settle for a low-skilled position. He didn't understand. We were free, provided for ourselves, and were restricted only by our energy and potentials. This was time for celebration!

Later we found out that in 1980, the last year of the Carter administration, the United States was in a bad recession. We couldn't tell. Apartments were available, food was plentiful, and department stores had a wide variety of products. We were in a land of abundance! We strived for a better life ahead. In about a year, I found an entry-level position as computer programmer, and Grigory enrolled into master's degree program at Johns Hopkins University. Martin Marietta covered his school expenses.

1981. Our first new car—a Dodge Omni.

### *Kidney Stones*

In our second year, Grigory had an attack of kidney-stones; this was the second time he experienced this painful attack. The first time was back in Russia. We were in the middle of our emigration process and therefore about to lose our jobs. On his last assignment as a field service engineer, Grigory experienced severe pain. Moaning and crouching, he hitchhiked his way home and called me, and we went to our designated clinic. After squirming from pain for a few hours in a waiting room, he was finally invited into the doctor's office. When he came out, paled and withered with a bag full of prescription pills, I remembered that my friend's father died from a medication overdose. I searched my home remedies book and found a recipe for a decoction in order to stimulate kidney stone passing. After several long painful hours, my husband got rid of his stone. Frightened by pain and helplessness and worried about our future, Grigory quit smoking. It was probably his tenth attempt, but this time it worked.

The American experience with kidney stones was different. When severe pain struck Grigory at work, a coworker drove him to the closest ER. Within half an hour, he was x-rayed and received an injection. He spent one night in the hospital where nurses periodically checked on him. In the morning the doctor prescribed a few pills and signed his release. I picked my husband up; he soon passed the damn stone at home and was at work next day. It was a good lesson in free versus pay-for-medical-care delivery systems.

## New Life

The year 1985, five years after we emigrated from the USSR, was milestone year for us. I always wanted to have three children, but it was too difficult to raise children in the USSR, so we had just one son. At the end of December 1984, thirteen years after our first child was born, we invited our second son to the world. In May 1985 Grigory graduated with a master's degree from Johns Hopkins. The same year we became citizens of the United States.

We wanted to be closer to my brother's family, the only relatives we had. After a job search in the New England area, Grigory found new job, and we moved to Connecticut. With a flattering letter of recommendation from my last job in Baltimore, I didn't have any problem also finding a new job.

In dramatic contrast to the way it was in the USSR, we could relocate without permission from authorities, and we didn't have any problems finding and renting an apartment. Despite our imperfect English, we were able to progress with no connections to the right people in the right places.

I wanted our sons, Len and Michael, to know more about Judaism so that their relationship with religion would be their own choice and not the government's. We started to read about Judaism, listened to tapes on the Bible by Dennis Prager, and introduced Jewish religious holidays to our home life. Our family also fully embraced traditional

American holidays. Thanksgiving and Independence Day are relevant and personal holidays to us. I love Christmas decorations, and when Christmas coincides with Hanukkah, a special, uniquely spiritual reality is created. I understand why some of the best Christmas songs, like Irving Berlin's "White Christmas," were composed by Jewish immigrants. There are not many places on Earth where Jews are not afraid to practice religion or simply be Jewish.

We celebrated holidays with our friends and fellow emigrants and often shared our experiences, especially funny moments mostly related to our imperfect English. The winner was one of our friends. She worked as a computer programmer. She invited her colleagues for a Russian-style dinner. After serving appetizers, she got up and proudly declared: "And now we will have the main intercourse!" The guests were stunned, and silence followed. Her husband came to the rescue.

## Collapse of "Grand, Powerful Soviet Union"

We never expected the USSR to crumble. We knew the Soviet economy was in shambles and couldn't compete with free-market systems, but the image of a powerful and monolithic society was ingrained in our minds.

"On the eve of the 1980s, instead of being able to proudly report surpassing the American economy, the Soviet leadership sat behind closed doors and read a top-secret report on the economy's failings," according to *An Autopsy of the Soviet Economy* by Hoover Institution scholar Gordon M. Hahn. "In December 1979, the Soviet government delivered a 126-page economic report to the party leadership detailing the economic, demographic, and social problems that needed to be resolved to avoid economic contraction. The report highlighted the enormous gap between Soviet economic performance and that of the United States and Japan and suggested that the Soviet economy would continue to stagnate until reforms were implemented."

Added James Graham in *Perestroika and the Soviet Economy*, "Gorbachev never planned to remake the Soviet system he merely wanted to modernize it. Minor adjustments he implemented were his attempts to discipline the work force with slogans calling for 'intensification and acceleration.'"

In the 1980s in order to slow down their economic disaster, the Soviets desperately needed trade with the capitalist countries. The strong anti-Communist stand of Pope John Paul II, Ronald Reagan, and Margaret Thatcher prevented the USSR from stopping the democracy movement in Poland, as they did in 1956 in Hungary and 1968 in Czechoslovakia. The democracy movement in Poland triggered a domino effect to other Eastern European countries under Soviet Communists control: Czechoslovakia, East Germany, Hungary, Bulgaria, and Romania.

American media often gives credit to Mikhail Gorbachev for the collapse, but Gorbachev did not orchestrate the dissolution of the USSR; he was just a figure taken down by the tsunami of collapsing Socialist economy, coinciding with people rising to freedom. Stagnation of the centrally planned economy in combination with people rising against concentrated power of Communists led to the dismantling of the USSR.

### Visiting Homeland

After the fall of the USSR, Russian borders were opened for visitors from abroad. Seven years after we immigrated, we could visit our relatives. Sadly, six months before the collapse of the USSR, my father was injected with wrong medication while at the hospital. He passed away three days later. He was seventy years old. Len was eight years old when we left Russia. During his second year in American school, he was given an assignment titled "My Life." He described how he looked through the window of our train leaving the station in Minsk and didn't understand why everybody was crying. Only later did he understand that he would never see his loving grandparents, cousins, and childhood friends again.

I stayed in America with our little son. Excited and anxious, Grigory and fifteen-year-old Len went to our motherland for a visit. The reunion was bittersweet. In terms of life-changing experiences, our seven years in the United States had different density. We had already bought a house and drove cars to work. Len had just started high school; he was thinking about what courses to take and what extracurricular activities to participate in to be accepted to a good college. We traveled on our vacations and holidays and had already seen more places than we ever could in a lifetime living in the USSR.

In contrast, there were not any changes in the lives of our loved ones. The places we used to live seemed tiny; everything and everybody looked worn-out and tired. People on the streets didn't smile, and in stores people were rude and aggressive. On third day of their visit, my poor guys had nightmares about not be able to return to America.

While flying back home, Len had an anxiety attack from the thought that his parents would not immigrate and he would still live in Russia. Several years later in the essay part of his college application Len described these horrifying thoughts. He was accepted to the University of Pennsylvania, the college of his choice; they indicated that his essay played a weighty role in his acceptance.

### Relatives Are Coming

With collapse of the Soviet economy, Soviet currency dramatically deflated; people's life's savings were wiped out, and places of work were in disarray. Anger and frustration led to ethnical blames. Anti-Semitism was openly aggressive. With our sponsorship, our relatives applied for emigration to the United States.

Adjusted to Soviet routine and not risk-takers, they had to discover that their destinies were in self-reliance. They started from jobs below their qualification and eventually moved up.

### What Is a Definition of the American Dream?

The difference between Socialism and capitalism is very clear.

Under Socialism, talented individuals are held down by envious mediocrity and indifferent bureaucrats. Lack of incentives and limited brain power of central government suppress initiative and slow down progress. Robed of individual choices and confined to assigned bounds, people lose aspiration, self-esteem, and dignity. Government-controlled, centrally planned society is a quagmire; in the quagmire your soul will slowly suffocate in warm, sticky sludge.

In capitalism, dynamic, unbound people in search of personal prosperity invent, create, and move progress forward, generating opportunities and higher standards of living for all. Despite all the hardship of surviving in the new culture—losing jobs, being insecure, finding new opportunities—we would never exchange this life back to the stagnant degrading life of Socialism. I don't even know how many cars we have had after our first used 1972 Dodge Coronet. We bought a house. Our children graduated from college. We travel a lot. We can see results of our efforts.

People often say that this is what the American dream is about. I disagree. We achieved our dream with our first step onto American soil. Our American dream was to be free.

# 8

# Cold War – Second Front

From our very first year in the United States, I was puzzled when people asked me, "Why did you immigrate?" It was disappointing to realize that so many Americans are uninformed and ungrateful for what they have. Socialist principles of equality were tested in the USSR from 1917 to 1987 and resulted in more than twenty million Soviet citizens killed. The rest lived in poverty and humiliation. Meanwhile, American intelligentsia is willfully oblivious to this reality. While millions of citizens were being killed and persecuted in the Soviet Union, children in Soviet schools were being taught about the greatness of Socialist society and unfairness of the capitalism. Unfortunately, the same theme is taught in American schools. It seems that American schools curricula were dictated by long-gone Soviet Communists. The history of Socialist countries is whitewashed of its brutality and failures for American students as it was for children in Soviet schools.

There are many YouTube videos dating from the 1980s about a professor who is a devoted critic of the United States. He defines himself as a libertarian Socialist or social anarchist. How nice it must be to be born in the United States, to be employed for fifty years at an American university, and to enjoy the security of that institution and protection of the community police department. How ironic it is to be protected by the nation's military forces and still call yourself an anarchist. Well supplied with food and other necessities, he lectures about the advantages of a society where private property is replaced with collective cooperatives as means of production, and audiences marvel at what he has to say.

As I listen to Democratic presidential candidates' rhetoric and

*Svetlana Kunin*

initiatives, I hear eerily familiar motives from our past. For many years we were surrounded with and studied the same ideas. They are using Marxists demagoguery to organize followers and insert an army of powerful soulless bureaucrats into every aspect of the citizens' life.

In the fall of 2008, at the height of the presidential campaign, my family and friends went to a small art movie house to see a documentary titled *Refusnink*. It was about the dissident movement in the USSR in the 1960s and 1970s—the same people who made it possible for us to emigrate. After the movie, the audience was asked to stay to hear words from the American Israel Public Affairs Committee (AIPAC) representative from Manhattan. The young lady made a short introductory speech about the committee and ended her speech with words promoting Barack Obama for president. The film showed how dissidents in search of freedom rose up against an oppressive central government. But here was the AIPAC representative urging us to vote for a candidate who vowed to transform America from a country of individual liberties to a country of centralized government. If it weren't so pathetically ignorant, it would be funny.

I realize that there is a history that explains this phenomenon. By the late 1950s, Soviet Communists realized that they could not overtake capitalist's free market economy of the United State. The goal to "reach and exceed gross domestic product of the United States" disappeared from subsequent Five-Year Plans of economic development of the USSR. However, in 1956, addressing Western ambassadors, Secretary General of the Soviet Communist Party Nikita Khrushchev declared: "Whether you like it or not, history is on our side. We will bury you". The second front of the Cold War—the insidious ideological war—intensified. This ideological war was not over when sclerotic Socialist economy of the USSR collapsed in 1991. The Soviet-style anti-American propaganda infiltrated the American educational system.

Progressives—ignorant admirers of Marxism/Leninism—are continuing the ideological war between capitalism and Socialism within the United States. They make late Soviet Communists very happy. Lenin, Stalin, Khrushchev, and following Communist leaders salute American progressives from hell.

# 9

# IBD Exclusive Commentary Series: Perspectives of a Russian Immigrant

## *Letter to the Editor*

In August 2009 I wrote a letter expressing my concerns and sent it around to local newspapers, some online sites, and publications we subscribed to. It read as follows:

> In the Union of Soviet Socialist Republics, I was taught to believe individual pursuits are selfish, and sacrificing for the collective good is noble. In kindergarten we sang songs about Lenin, the leader of the Socialist Revolution. In school we learned about the beautiful Socialist system, where everybody is equal and everything is fair; about ugly capitalism, where people are exploited and treat each other like wolves in the wilderness.
>
> Life in the USSR modeled the Socialist ideal. God-based religion was suppressed and replaced with cult like adoration for political figures. The government-assigned salary of the proletariat (blue-collar worker) was 30 percent to 50 percent higher than any professional. Without incentive to improve their lives, people drank themselves to oblivion.

*Svetlana Kunin*

Engineers, lawyers, doctors, and teachers earned a government-determined salary that barely covered the necessities, mainly food.

Raising children was a hardship. It took four to six adults (parents and grandparents) to support a child. The usual size of the postwar family was one or two children. Every woman had the right to have an abortion, and most of them did, often without anesthesia.

There is a comparative historical reality that plays out the consequences of two competing ideologies: life in the USSR and in America. When the march to the workers' paradise the Socialist Revolution began in 1917, many people emigrated from Russia to the United States.

In the USSR, economic equality was achieved by redistributing wealth, ensuring that everyone remained poor with the exception of those doing the redistributing. Only the ruling class of Communist leaders had access to special stores, medicine, and accommodations that could compare to those in the West. The rest of the citizenry had to deal with permanent shortages of food and other necessities and had access to free but inferior, unsanitary, and low-tech medical care. The egalitarian utopia of equality, achieved by the sacrifice of individual self-interest for the collective good, led to corruption, black markets, anger, and envy. Government-controlled health care destroyed human dignity.

Chairman Nikita Khrushchev released facts about Stalin and his purges. People learned of the horrific purge of more than twenty million citizens, murdered as enemies of the state.

Those who left Russia found a different set of values in America: freedom of religion, speech, individual pursuits, the right to private property, and free enterprise. The majority of those immigrants achieved a better life for themselves and their children in this capitalist land. These opportunities let the average immigrant live a better life than many elites in the Soviet Communist Party. The freedom to pursue personal self-interest led to prosperity. Prosperity generated charity, benefiting the collective good.

The descendants of those immigrants are now supporting policies that move America away from the values that gave so many immigrants the chance of a better life. Policies such as nationalized medicine, high tax rates, and government intrusion into free enterprise are being sold to us under the Socialistic motto of collective salvation.

Socialism has bankrupted and failed every society, while capitalism has lifted more people out of poverty than any other system.

There is no perfect society. There are no perfect people. Critics say that greed is the driving force of capitalism. My answer is that envy is the driving force of Socialism. Change to Socialism is not an improvement on the imperfections of the current system.

The slogans of "fairness and equality" sound better than the slogans of capitalism. But unlike at the beginning of the twentieth century, when these slogans and ideas were yet to be tested, we have accumulated history and reality.

Today we can define the better system not by slogans but by looking at the accumulated facts. We can compare which ideology leads to the most oppression and which brings the most opportunity.

When I came to America in 1980 and experienced life in this country, I thought it was fortunate that those living in the USSR did not know how unfortunate they were.

Now in 2009, I realize how unfortunate it is that many Americans do not understand how fortunate they are. They vote to give government more and more power without understanding the consequences.

There was no response from anybody.

Suddenly, three weeks later, I received a phone call came from *Investor's Business Daily* in California. "Hello, why did I send my letter to you? My husband has been a subscriber of yours for many years; I read your editorial pages and noticed an address for readers' letters." *IBD* not only ran my letter but gave me a forum, and "The Perspective of a Russian Immigrant" series was born. Following are columns I wrote during five years of the Obama presidency.

I feel that these articles are as relevant today as they were ten years ago.

*Russia Then, America Now*

Progressives' vision of a new twenty-first-century America reminds me of the seventy- year-old image of the Soviet Union. You could make a movie about traveling back in time. But it's not a movie.

Original publication date: October 30, 2009

**USSR, 1959:** I am a "young pioneer" in school. History classes remind us that there is a higher authority than their parents and teachers: the leaders of the Communist Party. The story of young pioneer Pavlik Morozov is required reading. Pavlik reported his father to the secret police for disobeying government regulations. His life exemplified the duty of all good Soviet citizens to serve their government.

From the first year in school, all of us are made aware of our ethnicity (ethnic Russian, Jewish, Asian, etc.) and class (proletariat, intelligentsia), around which society is structured. This inherent divisiveness makes it easy for the government to stir ethnic and class tension and in this way distract from economic failure. Newspapers and TV transmit government-approved news. Any critical voice is immediately suppressed and publicly denounced.

My parents, as all citizens of the USSR, work for state-run companies. All workers are unionized—another way the state controls the citizens. There is no private enterprise in USSR. Whatever small private farms or shops that existed before 1930 have been taken over by the state. All medical care and schools are state entities. The government regulates what kind of technology, service and compensation are allowed.

From school age through adulthood, citizens are called to public service four to five times a year. Activities such as farming, cleaning places of work, and paper/metal scrap collections are mandatory.

Religious symbols are forbidden in schools or on state property. Most old religious buildings are transformed for secular use.

The Soviet government imposes the Iron Curtain. The state has strict control over our ability to travel abroad. This prevents us from realizing the discrepancy between the media's image of the great socialist country and the reality of our low standard of living.

**USA, 2009:** "Progressives" control the government. Children in some public schools sing songs about the president and study his directives.

Progressives view people not as unique individuals, but as groups. They play on class envy, or divide people by ethnicity (African-American, white, Hispanic, etc.). From early childhood they remind children of their ethnic identity. The idea of a color-blind society united under the American flag is not politically correct.

The mainstream media are aligned with the government. Those media outlets critical of government policy are publicly criticized by government officials and are in danger of suffering repercussions.

Government seizes a majority stake in two major auto companies and, through TARP money, has control over major banks. Congress discusses capping salaries in private businesses and is in the process of increasing its control over the health care industry.

Big labor union leadership is fully aligned with the progressives in government. There is strong pressure to eliminate the secret ballot in order to increase union membership. Cap-and-trade, if passed, will drive a lot of small businesses into bankruptcy and create a fruitful soil for favoritism and government control over private entities.

Sept. 11 is declared a day of national service by the administration. It is no longer a day of remembrance for the horrific attack perpetrated by terrorists.

The American Constitution protects the separation between church and state. Atheist zealots pervert this ideal in order to force out religious symbols and traditions from public space. It is fashionable in progressive circles to ridicule religion and religious people. "Tolerance" is applied only to anti-religious values.

As a former citizen of the USSR, I heard and experienced all of this before. I listen to the speeches by the president asking people to sacrifice and serve. So what are we to sacrifice? For what? And to whom? I think I get it now.

Citizens of America sacrifice your elders and forget your selfish aspirations of prosperity for yourself and your family! Sign onto Service.gov and serve your government!

*Sacrificing for the Collective Good*

Original publication date: November 17, 2009

Whenever I speak about my experiences living in the USSR, my American friends respond that such things can never happen in a democracy like the United States. They don't understand why I am repulsed when I hear the president talk about "sacrificing for the collective good," which sounds so compassionate, as opposed to greedy capitalism.

"Sacrifice for the collective good" is one of the founding principles of socialism, where the collective, not the individual, is the basis of society.

Revolutionaries in Russia did not go around boasting about destruction; they made inspiring speeches about fairness, equality, justice and the greater good. After securing power and their own access to material goods, government officials decided what to give and take from the masses, according to their definition of what is good.

When party leaders talk about the "collective good," what they are really talking about is their right to determine what is good for the collective. Government bureaucrats decide what level of sacrifice is needed and who needs to sacrifice. They replace voluntary charity with the forceful redistribution of other people's private property.

Why do people born into a free society accept a failed 100-year-old ideology? It seems Americans are simply unaware of modern history. They don't know the theory behind slogans such as "fairness and equality" and "sacrifice for the collective good," much less how it works when implemented. They buy into old utopian slogans masquerading as new progressive ideals for "Hope and Change."

In the USA, people move up and down the economic ladder all the time. In Western Europe, a milder form of a socialist-democratic political system resulted in higher unemployment, less innovation and less social mobility compared with the U.S. European youth face a continuing decline in their standard of living, as they are burdened with an unsustainable welfare state.

In the USSR, China, North Korea and Cuba, a much harsher form of socialism led to mass murder and mass misery under the banner of "sacrificing for the collective good," "fairness and equality" and service to the state.

The USSR provides numerous examples of what an oppressive centralized government can lead to: Millions of talented artists, writers and scientists were sent to prison because they did not conform to government standards. Government control of agriculture led to constant shortages of food in one of the largest and most resource-rich lands in the world.

Americans think they are protected. The Constitution is a uniquely American document that specifically limits the power of the government and protects individual liberties. But if all branches of government will ignore this unique document, and people will allow them to do so, there will be nothing different about America.

Americans are not different from people in Russia, Germany, China, Korea or anywhere else. It is human nature to seek power and control, just as it is human nature to seek profit. Deny profit and you destroy any incentive for people to produce and innovate. Give up enough of your liberty to any centralized power and the result is entirely predictable.

Compare North Korea to South Korea, East Germany to West Germany before the fall of the wall—these are examples of the same people living under two different systems: socialism vs. capitalism.

Laws are necessary in a civil society, and this includes laws that regulate the free market. But a government takeover of the economy will result in the

*Svetlana Kunin*

transformation of the land of opportunity into a land of apathy and stagnation, a land in which individuals become cogs moving and turning according to government regulations.

In the USSR, they taught us in school that socialism is good and capitalism is bad. I find strange that they now teach the same in American schools.

## Who Are the People Who Support These Dictates?

Progressive's push for government control of medical care despite the citizens' outcry that raises the question: who are the people who support these dictates?

Original publication date: December 8, 2009

I look at the people who support the transformation of America in disbelief: They are destroying the very land that gave them so much opportunity. Groomed, well-fed and educated, comfortably living in a prosperous society, they need a mission to give meaning to their lives. These "fighters for the less-fortunate among us" glaze over the fact that hundreds of millions of people from around the world desperately try to come to this country for all it offers, regardless of their economic status, race, class, or gender.

Immigrants rightly see this country as the best place to obtain a decent life for themselves and their families. When I immigrated to America in 1980, I was overwhelmed with the amount of food and goods available at any store, at the numerous charitable organizations helping the needy, and even the government programs that helped people to obtain necessary skills to find a job. Later, I realized that the country was in the midst of a deep recession.

Compared to where I came from, it seemed like the pinnacle of prosperity.

As a secular Soviet Jew, my first Christmas in America was amazing. The proud display of religious symbols was a celebration not only of the holiday, but of a population free to express their beliefs without fear of oppression. I understand why at the beginning of the 20th century Jewish immigrants in America wrote many beautiful Christmas songs; these songs were born out of grateful hearts. Churches and synagogues coexist without issues. Nobody is forced to practice or not practice a religion.

Soon, however, I noticed darker aspects underlying life in America. Political correctness had seeped into everything like cancer. Under the pretense of multicultural diversity, suppression and intolerance of uniquely American traditions such as liberty, private property, and e pluribus Unum (out of many, one), became not only acceptable, but necessary in supposedly enlightened society.

Under the pretext of helping the needy, liberals eliminate people's drive to better themselves and their families. Instead, they obsess about events of the past and exacerbate the victim mentality in the very people they claim to help. The stranglehold of political correctness has only grown stronger. I see in today's governmental policies a replication of the very things I escaped from.

In the USSR, representatives of the Communist party—partorgs (literally: party organizers)—were ingrained into every aspect of civilian, official and military life. These political organizers controlled public order by observing the behavior and speech of every citizen. People who wanted a more secure and privileged life found it necessary to join the propaganda machine. In order to survive, citizens were silent out of fear of retaliation by the authorities.

Government-controlled medical care and poorly compensated medical personnel stimulated corruption at every level of service. People had to resort to bribery in order to get the help they needed, and underpaid medical personnel were open to the payouts.

Those who could not pay had to beg for help. The only hospitals comparable to American hospitals were in Moscow and a few other cities, where government officials were treated. In the rest of the country, medical care was substandard. This was the reality of free health care for everyone.

No one can dispute that America has issues with its medical system, and here too, some people struggle to get the help they need. But the solution to the problem is not more bureaucratic control. The quality of medical care will inevitably decline for everyone.

I came to this country in the middle of a recession, and I saw the economy revive and prosper when the government eased the tax burden on people and businesses. People were free to use their talents without the interference of central planning. Today the opposite is taking place, and we see the opposite results because central planning results in wasteful spending, corruption and the suppression of initiative.

I am afraid these transformers of America are destroying the future of our children. I hope the free spirit of America triumphs.

*Natural Laws*

Natural laws are part of the human social construct. In controlled societies concentration of power is inevitable, dissent is not acceptable, individualism and ingenuity are not encouraged, and corruption and cronyism replace entrepreneurship. It is much easier for the centralized government to deal with obeying followers, but they seldom have new ideas. That's why all Socialist countries are stealing and imitating new technology from the United States.

Original publication date: January 21, 2010

Visitors to national parks are warned not to feed the wildlife because this interferes with the natural survival ability of the animals. Progressives do not make the same connection with human nature.

The image of a country where government takes care of its citizens attracts the liberal mind. This image has two dimensions: fairness and equality. Many American intellectuals admired the Olympic opening ceremony last summer in Beijing: Hundreds of expressionless men moved and beat their drums in perfect unison, an impressive and symbolic image as, in real life, each man has an allocated and regulated place and function.

Hollywood liberals are impressed with Venezuela, where the evil capitalists are kicked out of the country and the government controls the media. Democratic congressmen admire the idea of the Cuban system. They ignore the fact that the government prohibits its citizens from leaving the country, and foreigners are allowed to see only what the government wants them to see.

Released Soviet archives show how a society can project an image of glory and prosperity, as long as the intended audience is shown only two dimensions. But they also reveal the third dimension: the dimension of cruelty.

In such societies, individuals, science, education, art and sport are subservient to ideology. There are numerous examples. A whole branch of

*Svetlana Kunin*

science—genetics—was eliminated for 20 years when party leaders declared it to be a bourgeois pseudoscience and a "whore of capitalism" because it contradicted the theory of Marxism-Leninism. Scientists were sent to labor camps or killed. Leading Soviet geneticist Nikolai Vavilov died in prison.

The control of mediocrity over talent is the defining structure of these societies. There are political rules. If you conform, then you are living among equals. If you break the rules, then you suffer. If you are part of the ideological machine, you are a beneficiary of the system. That is why there are former citizens who have fond memories of the USSR.

Such ideological oppression is insidious, and we increasingly find it in America. Already, American parents are forced to send their children to failing schools. Americans will soon find the same to be true of their medical care. Political correctness limits their speech and corrupts their actions, as was on display in the Fort Hood attack.

How can correctness be political? If it is political, then it is an agenda.

In contrast to the progressive vision, the strength of America is built on ideals such as individual liberty and the law of the land. These two dimensions gave life to the third dimension: opportunities.

Americans have the opportunity to make choices free from any centralized control. Free individuals have the opportunity to escape a bad situation, and explore their talents and aptitude. The American Constitution protects individuals from oppressive government.

How do our current political leaders propose to transform America? They ignore the Constitution. They will collect the income of citizens living today and those not yet born. They envision a zoo like country where the citizens are assigned a place to live, to work, the medical care they can get and the food they eat.

Our leaders will be our zookeepers, fairly distributing services and goods. People will rely on zookeepers and forget how to plan their own lives and take care of themselves.

The image of a fair and equal society will be projected, but the third dimension—a bureaucratic cruelty over defenseless individuals—will result. This is not a progressive society; it's an oppressive one. There is no escape from oppressive centralized state control.

Those who support this transformation cannot see beyond the flat two-dimensional image of utopia.

*Promises of Fairness and Equality*

When the Russian Revolution took place in 1917, the new Socialist ideals were fresh and appealing. Revolutionaries included believers of all stripes—from peasants to aristocrats. Young Jews from Pale of Settlement, including my parents, were among the believers. But the promises did not materialize. The destruction of the old order was followed by top-down control, disillusion, apathy, low standards of living, and, finally, searches for scapegoats. To redirect populous anger, the Soviet government insidiously steered up ethnical animosity, especially anti-Semitism.

Original publication date: February 2, 2010

There was an old Soviet saying: If you need to find food to fill your refrigerator, plug it into the microphone of a party leader giving a speech. Today in America, if we plug a refrigerator into our leader's teleprompter, I suspect the refrigerator will stop working. Democratic party leaders speak incessantly of limiting profits and regulating salaries.

*Svetlana Kunin*

It brings back to memory another Soviet line: You pretend you are paying us salaries, and we pretend we are working. If bureaucrats predetermine the value of your work, there is no incentive to be productive. This is the quickest way to kill a dynamic economy.

I never expected to hear this kind of rhetoric in the USA. Today, the American educational machine teaches exactly the same points the Soviets taught. It idealizes Socialist societies and denigrates America, especially its economic system. American students are brainwashed to despise economic freedom and to yearn for a big government state.

Freed from their parents' control, but intimidated by the relentlessly negative portrayal of America, young Americans look for politicians to show them the way.

As someone who experienced real government-approved anti-Semitism in the Soviet Union, I am amazed by the obliviousness of American Jews, the most fervent supporters of left-wing politics. They support a party that is obsessed with pitting one group against another, and that incessantly plays on envy and hatred for bankers, rich people, big business and doctors.

They fail to notice that the success of Jews, as well as other minorities, in the sciences, business and arts is directly correlated to their freedom from oppressive, centralized control. American Jews who support big government do not understand what their ancestors escaped from.

Persecutions of Jews throughout history all have one thing in common: a centralized power that manipulates and directs people's anger away from themselves onto an easy target. No matter how much

Jews align themselves with the power structure and work for noble causes, they will remain an easy target.

As they said in the Soviet Union pertaining to Soviet Jews: They don't beat your record; they beat your face—meaning that no matter how much you try to assimilate, no matter how many good deeds you do, the centralized power can direct populist anger toward you and crush you when it suits them.

When the Bolsheviks took power after the 1917 proletarian revolution, their first steps were to take control of the banks and the media. Of course, it is not fair to compare our current American democratic leaders with the Bolsheviks.

Yes, they both use the same slogans in their speeches.

Yes, they both stir up envy and class warfare to distract from their failures.

Yes, both political movements sought control of the banks as the foundation for their new egalitarian vision.

And yes, they are both opposed to free speech, as was made clear by the reaction of American leftists to the recent Supreme Court decision.

But you would never find a Czar anywhere in the Soviet government.

*Contemporaries*

The wave of the anti-American movement in the 1960s and 1970s in the United States coincided with the dissidents' movement in the USSR. But there was a big difference: the lives of the anti-American demonstrators in the United States were not in any danger. Void of appreciation for anything American, they were free to dispute and deface founding principles or government policies. Many of these activists made careers out of anti-American activities.

The opposite was true for Soviet activists. Dissidents paid for their antigovernment activities with their lives, careers, and futures, including the futures of their children.

Original publication date: March 8, 2010

People often ask me why I left the Soviet Union. The real question is: How is it possible so many Americans ask such an absurd question?

One seminal figure in the struggle for freedom in the USSR was Andrei Sakharov (1921–89), the leading figure in the development of the Soviet hydrogen bomb. A member of the Soviet elite, he enjoyed a better quality of life compared with most of his fellow citizens.

Yet he witnessed the grotesque treatment of citizens who dared question government policies. From the early 1960s, he became a leading spokesman for human rights in the Soviet Union. Sakharov saw the true nature of socialism: "This position of the intelligentsia in society renders senseless any loud demands that the intelligentsia subordinate its strivings to the will and interests of the working class (in the Soviet Union, Poland and other socialist countries).

"What these demands really mean is subordination to the will of the party or, even more specifically, to the party's central apparatus and its officials. Who will guarantee that these officials always express the genuine interests of the working class as a whole and the genuine interests of progress rather than their own caste interests?"

Sakharov's international prestige prevented party leaders from eliminating him. Under constant KGB surveillance, he was exiled in 1979 from his native

Moscow to Gorky, a city that at the time was closed to foreigners. He was able to return to Moscow in 1986.

Another courageous Soviet dissident was Natan Sharansky, born in 1948. He became actively involved in the fight for religious and intellectual freedom in the USSR, as well as the right to emigrate. After his arrest in 1977, he spent 16 months in solitary confinement and later was transferred to a Siberian prison camp.

In the same era that Soviet dissidents experienced the worst forms of oppression because of their fight for freedom of speech and the right to practice their own religion, American intellectuals such as Howard Zinn (1922–2010) wrote about how capitalist America was unfair compared with socialist countries.

Zinn had this take on history: "Objectivity is impossible and it is also undesirable. That is, if it were possible it would be undesirable, because if you have any kind of a social aim, if you think history should serve society in some way; should serve the progress of the human race; should serve justice in some way, then it requires that you make your selection on the basis of what you think will advance causes of humanity."

While Natan Sharansky and other Soviet dissidents were jailed in the Soviet Union, Chicagoan Bill Ayers (born in 1944) was involved with Students for a Democratic Society, an organization that found the Soviet model inspirational. This group evolved into the Weathermen—a communist, militantly anti-American group.

Did they not hear of Sakharov and Sharansky? They were far from the only ones to reveal what really went on behind the Iron Curtain in the society built on the theory of class envy and collective good.

The Welsh journalist Gareth Jones reported on the Holomodor, the centrally planned famine that killed millions from 1932 to 1933 in the Soviet Ukraine. Food and grain were confiscated from farmers in the name of the "collective good."

In 1963, "One Day in the Life of Ivan Denisovich" by Alexander Solzhenitsyn was smuggled to the West. This book revealed life in the Soviet gulag system, where millions of people perished.

In 1971, Soviet dissident Vladimir Bukovsky managed to pass to the West more than 150 pages that documented the use of psychiatric institutions for political prisoners in the USSR. Soviet authorities incarcerated Bukovsky for seven years, and he spent an additional five years in exile.

Meanwhile, Zinn, living a comfortable life in the capitalist USA, was busy writing anti-American history books. He was never persecuted or imprisoned for his anti-American views. Rather, he continued to teach, and his books, full of his fantasy propaganda, are a principle source of teaching material in American education. And Ayers is involved in designing curricula for American public schools.

"I wanted my writing of history and my teaching of history to be a part of social struggle," said Zinn. "I wanted to be a part of history and not just a recorder and teacher of history. So that kind of attitude toward history, history itself as a political act, has always informed my writing and my teaching."

After collapse of the USSR and the opening of KGB archives, more evidence of the true nature of a totalitarian socialist system was made available.

Today, as former Soviet republics move toward the free-market model of capitalism, Democrats in America are transforming this country around the concepts of social justice and the collective good, the defining principles that animate oppressive socialist societies.

Writing in the New York Times in 1968, Sakharov warned: "Intellectual freedom is essential to human society—freedom to obtain and distribute information, freedom for open-minded and un-fearing debate, and freedom from pressure by officialdom and prejudices. Such a trinity of freedom of thought is the only guarantee against an infection of people by mass myths, which, in the hands of treacherous hypocrites and demagogues can be transformed into bloody dictatorship."

*Mainstream Media*

In 1932, as people were dying in the USSR from starvation (Holodomor) caused by Stalin's agricultural policies of forced collectivization, Pulitzer Prize winner Walter Duranty wrote in the pages of the *New York Times* that "any report of a famine in Russia is today an exaggeration or malignant propaganda" and that "there is no actual starvation or deaths from starvation but there is widespread mortality from diseases due to malnutrition."

Today, when I read the *New York Times*, I sometimes feel that its correspondents and I live in different countries. While they did not see anything wrong with the USSR, they don't see anything good in the United States.

Original publication date: March 29, 2010

In a front-page article last week in the New York Times, "In Health Bill, Obama Attacks Wealth Inequality," David Leonhardt wrote: "For all the political and economic uncertainties about health reform, at least one thing seems clear: The bill that

President Obama signed … is the federal government's biggest attack on economic inequality since inequality began rising more than three decades ago."

I guess we did not get a message when we immigrated to the USA three decades ago. I know immigrants from Argentina, France, Cuba, Czech Republic, Russia. We all came to America practically with nothing. Within three decades, when according to Leonhardt economic inequality was rising in America, we all accomplished what is defined as the American Dream.

How come "economic inequality" did not affect us? I think we were lucky because we avoided all government efforts to provide for the poor. We all had one common story: We started from whatever job we could find to support our families. In my case it was a data entry position at $4.50 an hour. Then we worked our way up.

I know doctors who worked at the cash register while studying for the medical exam, engineers who worked as mechanics or maintenance technicians, and some of them worked up to the engineering career. We did not have any special treatment or exceptions. It was pure perseverance.

Did American medical care make it harder for us to succeed? In my case, being in America saved my life. I had a serious surgery 10 years after we came to America. The technology used for this surgery did not exist at that time in the Soviet Union.

Leonhardt writes: "Beyond the health reform's effect on the medical system, it is the centerpiece of (Obama's) deliberate effort to end what historians called the age of Reagan." I suspect a specific and very large part of 20th-century history is missing for this Ivy League graduate.

During the "age of Reagan," we, like millions of other legal immigrants, were able to establish a successful and happy life in America. We did it not because we took what belonged to low- or high-income people, but because we did not rely on anybody's help.

Because of the low taxes and low unemployment during the Reagan era, we had more money to finance our needs. We learned new skills, we opened or worked for small businesses, we bought houses and educated our children.

And because of Reagan policies of a strong America, the oppressive socialist Soviet empire collapsed. Ask citizens from countries freed from Soviet domination what they think about the Reagan era. Ask Germans, Czechs, Poles, Hungarians, Romanians, Estonians, Latvians, Lithuanians, Georgians.

Leonhardt continues: "Much about health reform remains unknown. ... Maybe the bill's attempts to hold down the recent growth of medical costs will prove a big success, or maybe the results will be modest and inadequate. ... the proper balance between the market and the government—remains unresolved."

Some more history study could help David Leonhardt. He can check out liberal government fiascoes right here in America, including and especially our current economic troubles due to government policies such as the Community Reinvestment Act. Or he may discover failure of government-managed public schools, public housing, welfare programs mismanagement, the corruption of the Federal Home Loan Mortgage Corp., known as Freddie Mac, etc. And now they want to experiment with the medical care?

Leonhardt ends his article as follows: "Above all, the central question that both the Reagan and Obama administrations have tried to answer—what is the proper balance between the market and the government?—remains unresolved. But the bill signed on Tuesday certainly shifts our place on that spectrum."

He is right—the bill will shift life in America. Until March 23, 2010, America was the only country where majority of the people, independently of their occupation or income, had timely access to the advanced medical technology, medication and care. This bill will change this American treasure of quality of life.

Exceptions in the bill for members of government and some special groups will create the class of chosen people and then the rest of us—the masses. Proportions will shift: A small group will have access to the quality care. And the layer of the government bureaucrats will regulate what medical care is allowed for the rest of us.

The taxation required to sustain the skyscraper bureaucracies will end a uniquely American social mobility—people moving from lower income to higher income as their skills, experience and talents are accumulated. American society will become equally poor.

Soviet citizens behind the Iron Curtain could not compare their lives in the socialist ideal of equality and central planning with the outside. An Internet search on "alcoholism in the Soviet Union" will demonstrate the unintended results of the centrally planned economic equality, where your value is determined by the government.

The reality is that, compared with any country, American people have higher standards of living. If David Leonhardt is not scared of the consequences of this bill, then he is living behind a self-imposed Iron Curtain.

The disgraceful and humiliating production of this health care reform played out by President Obama, Harry Reid, Nancy Pelosi, 219 Democratic congressmen and 59 Democratic senators brought to memory the following epigram:

"Surrounded by thin-necked leaders,
He plays with subservient half-wits.
Some whistle, some meow and whine,
Only he is one who scolds dictates and designs."

The Russian poet Mandelstam wrote this in 1933. It was about the governing apparatus of the Communist Party surrounding Stalin. These people worked long hours on all Stalin's initiatives. Each of these apparatchiks signed off on his policies, even though some caused the elimination of thousands of innocent people. They were students of Karl Marx. They were in process of creating a socialist society, the transitional stage to the communism.

For that epigram, Mandelstam lost his freedom. Economic equality requires total conformity.

Did you notice how President Obama scolded Supreme Court members at his State of the Union address? And how there is a media onslaught against everyone who does not conform to this Democratic government? The New York Times is not in danger of the Democratic President's displeasure.

## Opposition Media

"He who now talks about the freedom of the press goes backward and halts our headlong course toward socialism." (Vladimir Lenin, leader of the first Communist government in Russia)

Original publication date: May 18, 2010

Sen. Barack Obama delivered a commencement address at Connecticut's Wesleyan University that called for sacrificing in order to build a fair and socially just society.

"We may disagree on certain issues and positions," he said, "but I believe we can be unified in service to a greater good. I intend to make it a cause of my presidency.

Two years later, at this month's commencement at the University of Michigan, President Obama talked about the role of government as a solution to the problems facing America. He complained about a lack of civility in our public debate. "Throwing around phrases like 'socialist' and 'Soviet-style takeover' and 'fascist right-wing nut' may grab headlines," he said, "but it also has the effect of comparing our government, or our political opponents, to authoritarian and even murderous regimes."

The president's rhetoric mesmerized the students at Wesleyan and persuaded supporters to join his cause for change. But to me and other immigrants from socialist countries, this rhetoric sounded familiar.

American college students, in awe of their new leader and excited about ideals such as social justice, a fair society, equality and the transformation of greedy capitalist systems in which workers are exploited, do not realize these progressive ideas are identical to what students in socialist countries were taught 40 years ago in required classes such as "political economics" and "Marxist-Leninist dialectical materialism."

The pleasant platitudes that make up leftist rhetoric are not new. The policies and actions of this government are almost identical to what took place in countries moving toward socialism throughout the 20th century.

Government appropriation of banks, other financial institutions, medical care, education, natural resources and regulation of speech is what came of centralized power in young socialist societies, leading to totalitarian regimes such as those in the USSR, China, Cuba and North Korea.

When House Speaker Nancy Pelosi, other Democrats in Congress and the media portray critics of this government as racists, right-wing nuts, Nazis or terrorists, it is more than lack of civility; it is a deliberate, Soviet-style authoritarian tactic to impose conformity on people who happen to disagree with the government's definition of the greater good.

At his commencement address in Michigan, Obama said we have the option to get our information from any number of blogs, Web sites and cable news shows. This of course requires that we all agree on a certain set of facts to debate from, and that is why we need a vibrant and thriving news business that is separate from opinion makers and talking heads.

At his next commencement address at Hampton University in Virginia, Obama further aired his concerns about uncontrolled information, which: "becomes a distraction, a diversion. It's putting new pressure on our country and on our democracy."

It was much easier to manipulate and direct public opinion in the Soviet Union, where the state apparatus had complete control of all sources of information. Centralized government propaganda and draconian suppression of free speech created an enforced conformity no one could escape.

That is why Obama wants to regulate the Internet and cable news shows so they are "neutral" as defined by the government. The Soviets demonized the opposition as enemies of the people; American leftists simply define any opposition to them as racist or extremist.

"The press should be not only a collective propagandist and a collective agitator, but also a collective organizer of the masses," said Vladimir Lenin. "He who now talks about the freedom of the press goes backward and halts our headlong course toward socialism."

Young, educated graduates, born in the freest society, figure Obama is not a socialist; he is something new and somehow uniquely qualified to enact tired, old ideas that will result in a new, fair and equal society.

The Rev. Al Sharpton, in a recent sermon in Danbury, Conn., summed it up well: "Dr. King's dream was not to put one black president in the White House. The dream was to make everything equal in everybody's house. President Obama is in the White House to help us get there, but we're not there yet."

An old Soviet joke defines socialist equality as follows: If your neighbor has a cow and you do not, kill your neighbor's cow.

*Government Knows Better*

Progressives insist that the free market system doesn't work, but government plans and controls do. Democratic Party leaders and their pundits either don't know how this country evolved and progressed or they assume nobody knows.

Original publication date: July 7, 2010

In a speech he gave in Wisconsin on June 30, President Obama said: "We already tried the other side's ideas. We already know where their theories led us. And now we have a choice as a nation. We can return to the failed economic policies of the past, or we can keep building a stronger future. We can go backward, or we can keep moving forward."

For the Soviets, moving forward meant that with each consecutive five-year government plan the economy of the USSR would eventually surpass the American economy (the one Obama thinks has failed).

They could have succeeded: Russia has abundant natural resources and a well-educated populace, with a culture that's been in existence for far longer than the United States. The central government enforced these five-year economic plans with zero interference from members of the U.S. Republican Party or Fox News. Yet, they were about as successful in growing the economy as Obama's stimulus package has been in creating American jobs.

The idea is that government-appointed experts and officials know how to drive innovation, rather than people who make their own choices, and who have real expertise and experience in their chosen field.

In his Oval Office address, President Obama spoke about creating a clean energy future: "As we recover from this recession, the transition to clean energy has the potential to grow our economy and create millions of jobs—but only if we accelerate that transition. Only if we seize the moment. Even if we're unsure exactly what that looks like. Even if we don't yet know precisely how were going to get there. We know we'll get there."

In 1959 Soviet Chairman Nikita Khrushchev, after returning from a visit to the U.S., decided that the USSR had to increase its production of corn. All Soviet republics, from Belarus to Siberia, replaced the crop most appropriate to their soil and climate with corn, as directed by the ministry of agriculture. The following year, the corn crop was a failure, and there was a shortage of potatoes and grain for the population to eat.

There is a common theme crystallizing from Democratic leaders: Their policies are driven by their ideological vision and, in their own words, they don't have a clue about what to expect.

Sen. Christopher Dodd, speaking about his financial reform bill, said: "After great debate, we have produced a strong Wall Street reform bill that will fundamentally change the way our financial services sector is regulated. No one will know until this is actually in place how it works."

Speaker Nancy Pelosi, talking about health reform in March, said: "(This) is legislation for the future, not just about health care for America, but about a healthier America. But we have to pass the bill so that you can find out what is in it, away from the fog of the controversy."

The response of authorities to the catastrophic oil accident in the Gulf of Mexico illustrates how centrally controlled bureaucracy works. It is revealing to see how the federal government obstructs localities trying to save their states from disaster.

America is an advanced and prosperous country. The failed economic policies that Obama talks about somehow produced a dynamic economy, with opportunities available to more people than everywhere else in human history.

But liberal elites do not make the connection: They yell loudly about regulating capitalism and talk quietly about regulating speech, capping salaries, taxing incomes and creating bureaucracies in order to control everything and everyone.

Instead of relying on basic laws of economics and an understanding of human nature, they elevate socialist-style management based on the political economics of class warfare and central planning. The left believes that the Constitution and Bill of Rights are backward and out of date. Meanwhile, their new ideas for transforming America are based on old, unsuccessful concepts from Marx, [Friedrich] Engels and [John Maynard] Keynes.

The country I grew up in was filled with statues of the leader, his arm proudly extended, pointing toward a future where the life of all citizens would be framed within the boundaries of his vision.

I prefer the Statue of Liberty.


*Studying the History of the World's Evil*

Striving for superiority over the United States was at the center of postwar foreign policy in the USSR. Today, formal Communist apparatchiks occupy key positions in the Russian government. Often Democrats are replacing dangerous reality with wishful thinking. Their readiness for unilateral disarmament is scary.

Original publication date: February 15, 2011

Studying the history of the world's evil is disturbing. But being ignorant of reality—or worse yet, ignoring it—is dangerous.

In 2009, when Secretary of State Hillary Clinton presented the "reset button" to Russia's foreign minister, I wondered whether anyone in the Obama administration was aware that the goals of the Russian negotiator were the enforcement of regional influence and the demise of the USA.

If the true history of communism was taught in American schools, perhaps this administration would understand that the collapse of capitalism was and is part of the communist/socialist psyche.

Today, when President Obama and Secretary Clinton make loud statements about "immediate" changes in the government of Egypt, I wonder if they understand the history of the region as deeply as they understand Russian negotiating partners.

Even the history of World War II—the rise and fall of German National Socialism/Nazism, and the history of the anti-fascist resistance—is presented to the American people in a somewhat dim way.

Growing up in the USSR, where almost everyone had a family member who fought and was wounded or killed in the war, we learned about the Young Guard (Molodaya Gvardiya), a partisan organization made up of 15- to 18-year-olds, under the leadership of Oleg Koshevoy (1926–43). They fought the Nazis from 1941 until they were exposed and captured in 1943. We learned about multiple partisan groups, where children as young as 7 were part of the anti-Nazi resistance.

It is appalling to find an apologetic sentiment from 400 rabbis for George Soros' collaboration with Nazis against Jews. It is quite justifiable to examine Soros, who is personally financing multiple organizations to influence the Democratic Party, and who recently declared that in the current events in Egypt, "The main stumbling block is Israel."

It is easier to project an image of a noble and caring person to the ignorant while talking socialist platitudes. Only honest studies of world history will put light on the fact that in both Nazi Germany and socialist USSR, justifying the "common good" over respect for individual liberties led to the concentration camps.

Claire Berlinski, a contributing editor at City Journal, wrote "A Hidden History of Evil: Why Doesn't Anyone Care About the Unread Soviet Archives?" But not everyone reads City Journal.

Washington Post columnist Anne Applebaum reviewed "The Way Back," Peter Weir's new movie about Soviet gulags. "I haven't found any reviews, so far, that hail this as Hollywood's first gulag movie, perhaps because hardly anyone noticed that there weren't any before," Applebaum wrote.

"Weir told me," she continued, "that many in Hollywood were surprised by the story: They'd never heard of Soviet concentration camps, only German ones.' If you need to explain what a film is about,' the film is in trouble—and this one almost was. Weir had difficulties getting it distributed."

A few years ago, Laura Bialis' documentary "Refusenik"—about the triumph of Soviet dissidents and their exodus from the USSR—got very limited exposure. One can only hope that "The Way Back" will find a bigger audience.

A fellow immigrant of mine once said about coming to the USA: "I was not looking for paradise; I was trying to escape hell." Unfortunately, so many beneficiaries of life in the USA have a distorted view of their country and very shallow understanding of the life outside.

I did not hear Warren Buffett asking for his taxes to be raised 30 years ago, and I did not hear Bill Gates asking for government regulations at the inception of Microsoft. So while Buffet, Gates, Soros and Hollywood are busy raising money for the re-election of Barack Obama so he can complete his dream of transforming the USA, I am glad that there are people who love the American founding principle of individual liberty.

I just hope American school curricula will be changed sooner rather than later.

*Soviet Propaganda Would Fit in with the United States of Today*

Alignment of Democratic Party leaders and mainstream media reminds me of the Soviet Union, where newspapers, radio, and television propagated information authorized by government entities. The content also is very similar. All that is missing are agitation posters.

Original publication date: May 18,2011

The Obama administration and Democratic leadership could easily save some money by incorporating old Soviet propaganda posters to manifest their actions and vision.

In the USSR, the governing Communist Party directed and controlled all aspects of life and the economy. Today in the USA, political correctness is used by American progressives to control speech and to suppress undesirable criticism. In the USSR, speech-control played a major role in silencing the opposition.

The nuanced difference is that those who critique Obama administration policies are accused of being racists or bigots; in the USSR, individuals who criticized the government were described as spies or traitors

Today in the USA, class warfare is a constant component of the speeches made by the president and other leaders of the Democratic Party. As in the socialist USSR, entrepreneurs who are using their ideas, vision and energy to start businesses and generate jobs are presented as un-reconcilable enemies of the working people.

There is no country in the world where socialism brought more progress, a better standard of living and better opportunities for its citizens than what people in free-market countries experience. Nevertheless, the schools and media in the USSR lied about the superiority of socialism over capitalism, just as they do now in the United States.

Courts constituted another level of control and enforcement of government policies in the USSR. Genrikh Jagoda (1891–1938), soviet commissar of the interior and chief commissioner of state security, said: "Opposite to the capitalists/bourgeois courts, our court's decisions are not based on dogmatic laws, but are strictly justified by revolutionary sensibilities."

Today in the USA, the commissar's stand is reflected in the decisions of many liberal judges. Wisconsin County Court Judge Maryann Sumi issued this statement March 2011: "It seems to me the public policy behind effective enforcement of the open meeting law is so strong that it does outweigh the interest, at least at this time, which may exist in favor of sustaining the validity of the law."

The mainstream media dutifully assert Democratic Party talking points, educators preach about the greatness of socialism and the evils of capitalism, and all Judeo-Christian religious references are removed from the public space. Still, American progressives could easily reuse some Soviet propaganda visuals.

In the USSR, after all religious symbols and references were removed from schools and public places, images of the party leaders were ubiquitous in all official and public venues.

Democratic leadership labeled the Tea Party movement "extreme," and President Obama declared Paul Ryan's 2012 budget plan "radical." I used to live in a country where people who valued individual liberties and despised big government were considered "extreme," where any proposal to save the economy by using free-market solutions would be called "radical." This country was the USSR (1917 to 1991).

By 1950, citizens of the USSR were afraid to express their opinions, and rarely objected or critiqued any government regulations. Independent thinkers with even the slightest objection to government directives were sidelined or removed from society. Their knowledge, experience, talents and ingenuity were lost.

People of East European socialist countries, controlled by the Communist Party of the USSR, yearned for a freer society. In 1956, the Soviets crushed the spontaneous revolt of Hungarian people against socialist policies imposed by the Soviet Communist Party. More than 2,500 Hungarians were killed. In 1968, thousands of the Soviet troops entered Czechoslovakia to stop the liberation and decentralization of their economic system from the rigid, centrally controlled socialist structure imposed on the Czechs by the USSR.

In 1980, a nongovernment anti-communist union was organized in Poland. The Solidarity movement was joined by millions of citizens of all straits. They demanded liberty from the socialist government oppression. The Soviet media called them "extreme elements."

The alignment of three great leaders—Pope John Paul II, Ronald Reagan and Margaret Thatcher—who clearly understood the true inhuman and degrading nature of socialism made it possible for survival and eventual success of Solidarity. And by the end of 1990, the inefficient, unproductive, inhuman, centrally controlled socialist economy of the USSR collapsed. The Chinese communist government, witnessing the collapse of the USSR, introduced elements of capitalism into its economy.

Today, the dynamic capitalist society of the USA, driven by the individuals' ingenuity, is being replaced by the regressive socialist model of the government mandates, used in the USSR more than 80 years ago. President Obama and his supporters call it "Moving America Forward."

Timid Republicans, who compromise on the destructive or failed government programs, and who vote for judges in the image of old Soviet commissars, will not reverse the course. To restore the USA, it will take gutsy patriots to stand up to the progressives' propaganda attacks.

*Foreign Leaders Indicate Their Preferences*

As Barack Obama seeks reelection to a second term, some foreign leaders have already indicated their preferences. Informed and experienced Russians prefer a weak president who easily gives up advantages Americans have. Leaders who recognize evil of the world prefer a strong America.

*Svetlana Kunin*

Original publication date: July 8, 2011

"I can tell you directly," Russian President Dmitry Medvedev said in a June 19 interview with the Financial Times, "I would like Barack Obama to be re-elected president of the United States maybe more than someone else. … If another person becomes U.S. president, then he may have another course."

A month earlier, Lech Walesa, former leader of Poland's Solidarity union, declined an invitation to meet with America's president. "It is tough to tell journalists what you would want to tell the president of a superpower," Walesa told Poland's public broadcaster, TVP. "But this time I will not tell him, I will not meet him, the meeting does not suit me."

Obama is the product of teachings that both Medvedev and Walesa know well. To anyone who has lived in a socialist country, the class-warfare theory in Obama's rhetoric sounds all too familiar. Medvedev realizes that with the Obama administration, Russia has a good chance to return to its lost status of a powerful and feared nation, while the U.S. will continue to slide in a weak and hopeless direction.

From 1919 to 1991, the Soviets provided monetary support to help leaders of the Communist Party USA (CPUSA) and other Soviet sympathizers spread socialist ideals and anti-American propaganda.

In 1993, after the collapse of the USSR, experts from the Library of Congress traveled to Moscow to review previously secret archives of the CPUSA, sent to the Soviet Union for safekeeping by party leaders. The records revealed an irrefutable link between Soviet intelligence and the CPUSA.

On Dec. 2, 1939, Jay Lovestone, a founder of the CPUSA who had broken with the Stalin regime, testified before the House Special Committee about communist activities in the U.S.: "You cannot fight Stalinism in this country, or elsewhere, by repression, by outlawing legislation, by declaring it a crime to be a member of it. When you do that, you supply them the most powerful sentiment—blood of martyrdom.

"Secondly, I think their ideas ought to be subjected to maximum sunlight. They represent a special type of character, and I am convinced, in the light of their own traditions and the light and the character of the labor movement, that if their ideas are subjected to the opening, scorching sunlight and sunshine, that they cannot flourish."

Today in the U.S., Lovestone's advice is forgotten. The investment by the old Soviet commissars, from Lenin and Stalin to Khrushchev and Brezhnev, in the socialist and anti-American propaganda inside the U.S. has paid off.

Proponents of a big and powerful government that regulates the lives of others are reminiscent of the Japanese soldiers who continued to fight years after their country surrendered to end World War II in 1945. American liberals and progressives are oblivious to the fact that socialized economies either collapse (USSR), go bankrupt (Europe) or keep people locked in poverty (Cuba, North Korea, African nations).

The so-called American elite, supporters of the Obama administration, have much in common with the Soviet "nomenclatura"—those within the USSR and other Eastern European countries who held key administrative positions and regulated all aspects of people's lives but were themselves excluded from the rules.

Last January, on the 100$^{th}$ anniversary of Ronald Reagan's birthday, a statue was unveiled in Budapest

*Svetlana Kunin*

by grateful Hungarians who honored his leadership in helping end communism. And on July 1, Reagan was presented posthumously with the highest Czech state decoration, the Order of the White Lion, for his contribution to communism's demise in Central and Eastern Europe.

America's real elite are people who appreciate the uniqueness of a country where government's power is limited by its founding laws, and achievements are not limited by the destructive consequences of the socialist agenda.

Barack Obama is bringing to America what people in former socialist countries experienced and rejected. Obama is reversing everything good about the U.S.—opportunities and prosperity inside and alliances with democracies outside.

That is why Lech Walesa, the legendary Polish anti-communist, declined to meet with Obama, and why Russia's Dmitry Medvedev is hoping for his re-election.

## Democrat Strategies Right Out of V. I. Lenin's Playbook

Vladimir Lenin provided many recommendations on strategic and tactical maneuvers for the implementation of revolutionary ideas. The pamphlet "Left-Wing Communism: An Infantile Disorder" (Russian: Детская болезнь "левизны" в коммунизме) is one of the most detailed tutorials. For my article I used the Russian source and translated its title as "Children's Maladies of the Left in Communism." It's the same work, just a different translator.

Original publication date: October 12, 2011

Vladimir Lenin, leader of the socialist revolution in Russia, published multiple tutorials for like-minded revolutionaries around the world. Someone in the Obama administration must be familiar with his writings. Socialist minds think alike.

In the "Children's Maladies of the Left in Communism/Results of the Popular Conversation About Marxists Strategy and Tactics" (V.I. Lenin, 1920), Lenin wrote on the critical importance of timing: "To accept the fight, when it is beneficial to your opponent, is a crime; and leaders of the revolutionary class who cannot maneuver, manipulate and compromise to avoid obvious defeat are useless."

According to Lenin's rule, it is strategically appropriate for President Obama to halt all policies that are inconvenient to his election. That's why regulations like the EPA ozone plan, which would impose tremendous regulatory burdens on manufacturing in the USA, and the full-blown implementation of Obamacare, will wait until after the presidential election of 2012.

Lenin also wrote on the importance of taking advantage of every available disagreement among opponents: "To win over a stronger opponent requires tremendous effort, the necessity of very careful, skillful use of any little crack among the opponents … requires the use of every available case to gain an ally—even if temporary, weak, unreliable or conditional."

It is interesting to observe how the avalanche of attacks against the Tea Party activists by mainstream media, liberal commentators and other Democratic Party representatives makes some Republicans uncomfortable with the Tea Party. Conservatives should realize that there is no time for old-fashioned political rituals when the transformation of the country is under way.

On using a society's democratic conventions to make that society weak, while increasing the power of the central government, Lenin wrote: "Participation in the bourgeois-democratic parliament not only doesn't hurt the revolutionary proletariat, but makes it easier to prove to the uninformed masses that this kind of parliamentary governing should be destroyed, helps in the success of distractions and helps in the elimination of the bourgeois parliaments."

Lenin was talking about the British system of government, but his main point was on the strategy of replacing democratic system of governing with centralized power. The theme of "broken government" is popular among liberals so much so that the governor of North Carolina, Bev Perdue, recently said: "I think we ought to suspend, perhaps, elections for Congress for two years and just tell them we won't hold it against them, whatever decisions they make, to just let them help this country recover."

Peter Orszag, former director of President Obama's Office of Management & Budget, wrote an article titled "Too Much of a Good Thing—Why We Need Less Democracy." Top mainstream Democrats such as Purdue and Orszag are in alignment with Lenin's teachings.

But while propaganda, deception and manipulation work on people, they do not work on economies. In 1920 Lenin forecast that the full transformation of the Russian society into the prosperous communist state would be completed by 1930–1940. By 1930, after the destruction of private manufacturing and the collectivization of the agriculture, the country was facing famine and hunger. After Lenin's death in 1924, Stalin continued centralizing power and silencing opposition. By

1937, travel outside the USSR was strictly regulated. People were locked inside the country, surrounded by government-controlled propaganda.

After Stalin's death in 1953, the next party leader, Nikita Khrushchev, declared that by 1980 the foundation of the communism in the USSR would be built. At the XXII summit of the Communist Party of the USSR in October 1961 he announced: "This generation of Soviet people will live in the communist society." By 1990, Soviets witnessed their economy, managed by government bureaucrats, collapse.

The disoriented "Occupy Wall Street" protesters, looking for a society where the government takes care of citizens and redistributes wealth, would find such a society in the USSR. Since that society collapsed, they can now look to North Korea or Cuba as the natural endpoint they're agitating for.

In an Aug. 8 speech, Obama said: "For all of the challenges we face, we continue to have the best universities, some of the most productive workers, the most innovative companies, the most adventurous entrepreneurs on Earth … What sets us apart is that we've always not just had the capacity, but also the will to act—the determination to shape our future; the willingness in our democracy to work out our differences in a sensible way and to move forward, not just for this generation but for the next generation."

There are plenty of countries around the globe with the capacity and will to act. There were plenty of capable and willing people in the USSR determined to shape their future. Many of them were trying to immigrate to the USA. What sets the United States apart are its founding principles, based on the concept of individual liberty and the protection of the private property. "The best universities, some of the most productive workers, the most innovative companies, the most adventurous entrepreneurs on Earth" that Obama mentioned are the result of these principles.

The fawning media, the divorced-from-reality professors, the crony capitalists and the power-hungry individuals do not set this country apart from any other. What does make the United States unique is the phenomenon of the Tea Party: freedom-loving people, rising against government interference into their lives.

It is no wonder that those who would like to transform this country despise Tea Party activists. Intentionally or not, the ideology of today's Democrats is closer to Lenin's writings than to the founding documents of this country.

*Occupy Wall Street Demagoguery*

When we immigrated to the United States in 1980, we came to a classless society. It was not an American custom to ask how much one earns. High earners could get fired, and low earners could get promoted. We were in the lowest bracket when we started our life in the USA and moved up. What's wrong with that?

Original publication date: October 31, 2011

Old-time Socialist leaders, the ruling 1% in the USSR, would be jealous of the Internet snitch sites set up by the administration. And the ability to corral herds of mindless followers using online social sites is a great achievement of the modern American Left.

The old-time socialists had to rely on snail mail to report on colleagues and neighbors. They had to travel and imbed agitators in local communities in order to organize. They developed merciless strategies and propaganda to make 99% of the population surrender their liberties and became servants of the state.

The "Occupy Wall Street" crowd is an amazing sight in the middle of Manhattan in New York. According to these modern-day "revolutionaries," if you do not belong to the 1% of "millionaires and billionaires," then you are the part of the 99% abused by capitalist society. The only way to fix this inequality is to join forces to eliminate unjust wealth distribution.

As an immigrant from a socialist country, I for some reason don't feel abused by the 1% of American "millionaires and billionaires." Instead, I feel lucky to live in the USA.

Countries in which the population is divided into the 1% and 99% exist. I emigrated from such a country. There, the 1% of the rich were represented by the group, who, in the name of the faceless masses (the collective good), had control over the lives of 99% of the people.

The result: 99% of the citizens in such countries are powerless to change anything in their lives, and subsist on an income lower than most welfare checks in America.

I do not see this country divided into two groups (the 1% vs. the 99%). While poverty indeed exists in the USA, most people at least have the opportunity to improve their lives. And even in America, it is government control that has led to impoverished communities. Incompetent government interference into the dynamic free-market economy has an extremely negative effect on the economy and, as a result, on the life of the middle class. Dazed "occupiers" are lemmings, willfully marching their way to serfdom. They repeat the sound bites of their invisible puppet-masters, whose goal is to create the 1%-99% society.

It is not a coincidence that totalitarian regimes around the world, like China, Iran, Venezuela and their acolytes within American society, such as the Socialist Party USA, endorse Occupy Wall Street.

It's no wonder that the anti-Semitic motives are part of this movement. Anti-Semitism is an ever-present component of totalitarian regimes, and is used to redirect the attention of the mob from failing policies of the government.

There is no parallel between the Tea Party and the Occupy Wall Street movements. There is no parallel in the fight to save liberty for this and future generations of Americans and the march to serfdom.

*Who Created Prosperity? Bureaucrats or Individuals?*

President Obama insists that the free market "doesn't work" and "never worked." In January 2012, in a posh Swiss resort of Davos, host of the World Economic Forum Klaus Schwab repeated the tune: "Capitalism in its current form has no place in the world around us."

Original publication date: December 19, 2011

I am not sure what is more puzzling: President's speech in Osawatomie, Kan., on Dec. 6, or the enthusiastic reviews in the mainstream media, such as "Obama attacks Republican economic theory: 'It's never worked,'" by Ann Kornblut in the Washington Post.

Talking about his grandparents and Americans of the past generations the president said: "They believed in an America where hard work paid off, responsibility was rewarded and anyone could make it if they tried—no matter who you were, where you came from, or how you started out. ... These values gave rise to the largest middle class and the strongest economy the world has ever known."

Past generations were right. When we immigrated to the U.S. in 1980, my family personally experienced the real opportunities that the country provided us.

President continued: "For most Americans, the basic bargain that made this country great has eroded. ... In 2008, the house of cards collapsed. We all know the story by now: Mortgages sold to people who couldn't afford them or sometimes even understand them. ... Banks and investors allowed to keep packaging the risk and selling it off. Huge bets—and huge bonuses—made with other people's money on the line. Regulators who were supposed to warn us about the dangers of all this, but looked the other way or didn't have the authority to look at all."

Why were mortgages sold to people who couldn't afford them? Why had regulators "looked the other way"? The president explained: "It combined the breathtaking greed of a few with irresponsibility across the system. ... Now, in the midst of this debate, there are some who seem to be suffering from a kind of collective amnesia."

Today, in the words of the president, "Children might not have a chance to climb out of that situation and back into the middle class, no matter how hard they work."

In her ravishing reaction to the president's speech, Kornblut writes, "Obama deployed the language of right and wrong, fairness and unfairness, in a lengthy address that aides said he largely wrote himself."

Who put obstacles in the way of American children? Who broke the process, which was

*Svetlana Kunin*

instrumental in the creation of the most prosperous middle class "where hard work paid off, responsibility was rewarded, and anyone could make it if they tried"? Maybe progressive elites are suffering from collective amnesia.

Government interference into bank mortgage practices was the primary cause of the sub-prime mortgage crisis. The Carter administration initiated the process, the Clinton administration amplified the practices and the "compassionate conservative" Bush administration further enabled and witnessed the practice to its crushing end.

More federal government interference into schools resulted in a worsening quality of education. Before the federal Department of Education was created by President Carter in 1980, American schools were ranked among the best in the world. Today U.S. scores are behind those of most other developed nations.

The government's War on Poverty did not eliminate poverty, but it did create more social issues. For many people, dependence on government handouts resulted in the loss of ability to search for the personal talents and aspirations.

Obama complains that "huge advances in technology have allowed businesses to do more with less," adding that "if you're someone whose job can be done cheaper by a computer or someone in another country, you don't have a lot of leverage with your employer when it comes to asking for better wages and benefits—especially since fewer Americans today are part of a union."

At the dawn of the Industrial Revolution at the end of 18th and the beginning of the 19th century, labor unions explicitly objected to and vandalized new technology for the fear of losing jobs. Unions, in order to protect their interests, consistently hinder progress and competition.

"Finally," the president said, "a strong middle class can only exist in an economy where everyone plays by the same rules, from Wall Street to Main Street." Perhaps President forgot about the fact that members of the government are excluded from the Patient Protection and Affordable Care Act (ObamaCare)? Or that Congress is exempt from insider trading laws?

In his speech President warned: "At stake is whether this will be a country where working people can earn enough to raise a family, build a modest savings, own a home and secure their retirement." Kornblut writes: "Although the unemployment rate has been a constant shadow hanging over Obama's presidency, the mechanics of job growth had only a small part in the speech, which dwelled as much on the need for infrastructure investments, better education and a tax code that Obama said 'must reflect our values.'"

This poses the question: Whose values? There is nothing new or innovative in rhetoric about investments into infrastructure and education, and "fair" taxation. In 1920 Vladimir Lenin, the first leader of the Socialist Society, declared: "Communism is Soviet power plus electrification of the whole country."

Of course, in America we are talking about different infrastructure projects, but the idea is the same. The slogan, "Study, Study, Study—as bestowed by the great Lenin!" was found hanging in each school in the USSR.

The question of a fair approach to taxation in totalitarian socialism can be simple. What is the minimal cost of living? The socialist answer can be found in the old Soviet joke: "The minimal cost of living is the minimum needed for people to live on, so that the government can be comfortable."

Whether talented or mediocre, proletariat or professionals, all were equally poor, while top government officials had special housing, stores and medical facilities allocated just for them. Education does not lead to a prosperous society if people are not free to pursue their interests.

The USSR lasted from 1917 to 1987. Despite the Russian population being very well-educated and everyone paying whatever government found to be "fair share" of their salaries, by 1987 the centrally managed economy was collapsing.

So what is it that drove American progress if, in the words of Obama, the free market "doesn't work. It's never worked"? Was America's standard of living achieved due to individuals using their own capacities, in their own pursuits for happiness or success, unhindered by government control? Or was it thanks to government bureaucrats drawing up plans and managing the economy?

American progressives remind me of the top echelon of Soviet Communists: so confident in their condescension to people outside their circle, so in love with their rhetoric about fairness and the welfare of the masses, and so indifferent to the real fate of individual human beings.

*Liberals' Views on Family Just Like USSR's*

Original publication date: April 18, 2012

"There was a time when the isolated, firmly-knit family, based on a church wedding, was equally necessary to all its members. If there had been no family, who would have fed, clothed and brought up the children? ... The customs and moral principles of family life are changing as the general conditions of life change. ... How can one talk of parents when the mother and father are out working all day and cannot find the time to spend even a few minutes with their children? ... It is not surprising therefore that family ties should loosen and the family begin to fall apart. The circumstances that held the family together no longer exist. The family is ceasing to be necessary either to its members or to the nation as a whole. ... The state is responsible for the upbringing of children."

These words are strikingly in step with modern-day progressive thought in the United States. But they were written in 1920 by Alexandra Kollontai in the USSR: "Women's Role in Production: Its Effect Upon the Family" (Selected Writing of Alexandra Kollontai, Allison & Busby, 1977. Translated by Alix Holt).

Kollontai, a Russian revolutionary and the first female Soviet ambassador to Norway, wrote: "Capitalism has placed a crushing burden on woman's shoulders: it has made her a wage-earner without having reduced her chores as housekeeper or mother. Woman staggers beneath the weight of this triple load. ... Under capitalism children were frequently, too frequently, a heavy and unbearable burden on the proletarian family. Communist society will come to the aid of the parents. In Soviet Russia the Commissariats of Public Education and of Social Welfare are already doing much to assist the family. ... The state does not need the family, because the domestic economy is no longer profitable: the family distracts the worker from more useful and

*Svetlana Kunin*

productive labor. The members of the family do not need the family either, because the task of bringing up the children which was formerly theirs is passing more and more into the hands of the collective."

Kollontai ends this writing with a passionate vision of the future: "Communist society wants bright healthy children and strong, happy young people, free in their feelings and affections. In the name of equality, liberty and the comradely love of the new marriage we call upon the working and peasant men and women to apply themselves courageously and with faith to the work of rebuilding human society, in order to render it more perfect, more just and more capable of ensuring the individual the happiness which he or she deserves. The red flag of the social revolution which flies above Russia and is now being hoisted aloft in other countries of the world proclaims the approach of the heaven on earth to which humanity has been aspiring for centuries."

Kollontai (1872–1952) lived long enough to see that nothing close to her imaginary "heaven on earth" realized. Her words that "woman staggers beneath the weight of this triple load" came true, except that they were very true in the life of Soviet women. One cannot compare the load and life of the average woman in the Socialist country to the load and life of women in the USA. I can judge—I was one of the working Soviet women and then one of the working American women.

Kollontai, as many revolutionaries, believed that the family unit will eventually dissolve. But after decades of experimenting with the open relationships in the USSR in the Twenties and Thirties, it was clear that family is the optimal arrangement for survival of human beings.

It took violent revolution and elimination of tens of millions of people to change culture in the republics of the USSR. They destroyed all religious institutions so any religious traditions and influences were eliminated. They replaced the Ten Commandments with the Moral Code of the Builder of Communism. Still, the family as the unit of the society could not be destroyed.

Amazingly, liberals and progressives in the capitalist countries found the way—welfare. When it's not a necessity for a healthy person to put in any effort to stay alive, why sweat? For a single parent, the more children you have, the more welfare you get. Why then get married? More and more welfare will produce fewer and fewer families. As Kollontai said almost a hundred years ago, "the task of bringing up the children which was formerly theirs is passing more and more into the hands of the collective."

Interestingly, there is no welfare in socialist countries. In the USSR people who didn't work could be imprisoned for parasitism (in Russian: тунеядство [tuneiadstvo]). In spite of the fact that in such countries everybody works, bureaucracy and welfare-like compensation are choking any productive energy, hence wealth is not produced.

Liberals overlook the fact that you need wealth to provide welfare. Therefore, as it is in Europe today, as wealth is spent welfare states collapse.

I have an idea why it's so important to the Obama administration to insist on free distribution of birth control and abortion pills. As his vision of society evolves, private decisions are replaced by government mandates; family intimacy and dignity are replaced with the authority of the government involvement; confident and unique individuals, required to create independent and productive families, are disappearing. How many children can the Obama administration provide for?

*Obama's Slogan "Forward" Is Used by Socialists Too*

Original publication date: May 15, 2012

There is a modern parallel to Obama's new campaign slogan, "Forward!" It is the motto of the modern Socialist Movement "Forward!" (translated: "Vperiod!"), founded in Russia in 2005. Its declared goal is the socialist transformation of society.

In March 2011, the Socialist movement Forward officially merged with another organization, Socialist Resistance, to create the Russian Socialist movement. Its website states that the organization provides a joint platform for the anti-capitalist left. As declared in the movement's Manifesto, the key task is taking anti-capitalist positions and comprehensive support for all forms of worker resistance to the power of the rich. The movement's main collaborative forces are trade unions, eco-socialists, gender equality movements, strike committees and protest-coordinating counsels. These are similar to President Obama's support groups: organized labor unions, environmentalists, feminists, community organizers and policy development organizations such as the Center for American Progress.

One component that the Obama administration has but the out-of-power Russian Socialist movement does not is an opponent-monitoring apparatus such as Media Matters—what Communist Party leaders in the former Soviet Union used to have.

After introducing the motto "Forward!"—identical to slogans of Socialists of the past and present—Obama rolled out an imaginary vision of Julia, in which the government is involved in all aspects of a person's life.

No need for virtual reality. There is a real-life timeline for an average person in a society where the government plans, regulates and provides free services for its citizens in countries past and present—the USSR, Cuba, etc.:

Government provides free education, free medical care and other services to all citizens by paying all working men and women salaries that allow for a certain minimal standard of living.

Children as young as a year old are enrolled in free day-care centers. There, they learn that for everything good in life, they should be grateful to the great party leaders, especially to the leader of the governing party.

At age 17, after graduating from the public high school and passing competitive acceptance tests, teenagers can enroll in free colleges and universities. But government-imposed quotas regulated certain ethnicities out of enrolling in specified occupations.

Unless someone from the family is a member of the government with access to special clinics, hospitals and the best doctors, a person in need of medical attention visits a free clinic assigned to his or her address and waits in line to see a doctor assigned to the clinic.

If surgery is required, it is performed free of charge in overcrowded hospitals, with reusable surgical instruments. Due to a lack of medication, especially at the hospitals outside capital cities, minor surgeries are performed without anesthesia and with limited painkillers, followed by recovery amid unsanitary conditions with little attention from nurses.

After graduating from college, new professionals are assigned their places of work. Independent of occupation, their salaries are just enough to cover bare necessities, as was the case for their parents.

When young adults get married, they can afford to have one child. Two children is a stretch. A family with just one child would not be able to live on one salary. Due to shortages of contraceptives, abortion is a common birth-control mechanism and, as with all minor surgery, often performed without anesthesia. At retirement, most citizens live on pensions below a minimal standard of living.

I personally lived that life in the former USSR until age 30. When my young family of three immigrated to the USA, my parents stayed behind. After botched medical procedures in a free hospital, my father screamed from pain for three days before he died at age 70.

There's a lot in common among a Democrats' administration striving for total government involvement in people's lives and the communists of the former Soviet Union.

The society that Obama is moving America "forward" will allow any president to outlaw or impose whatever he wants without consent of the people.

*Why ObamaCare Won't Work*

Original publication date: July 5, 2012

In defending the expansion of Medicaid as part of the Affordable Care Act (ObamaCare), Supreme Court Justice Elena Kagan argued that the government will provide states with the necessary money: "It's just a boatload of federal money for you to take and spend," she said. Her fellow Supreme Court judges reinforced the notion that "a boatload of federal money" comes from taxation.

I came from a country where everyone had guaranteed access to free medical care, which was paid for by confiscatory taxes imposed on working people. There is a physical limit on how much you can squeeze from people in taxes. Consequently, government-guaranteed services become strictly regulated and limited. In the USSR, taxpayers and their families faced low-quality medical care, medication shortages and overcrowded hospitals with outdated technology, while government officials had access to the best hospitals. That anyone in the United States will support similar model is beyond comprehension.

The Supreme Court also decided that if the government doesn't want to protect the country's borders, states do not have the authority to do anything dealing with a large illegally migrating population of humans. Who are the people who support these policies of expanded central control?

In his New York Times column, correspondent Thomas Friedman said: "One-party autocracy certainly has its drawbacks. But when it is led by a reasonably enlightened group of people, as China is today, it can also have great advantages. That one party can just impose the politically difficult, but critically important policies needed to move a society forward in the 21$^{st}$ century."

What about this in the Bangkok Post: "China said … it was investigating the case of a woman who was allegedly forced to abort seven months into her pregnancy, after images posted online of the baby's corpse caused an uproar" (June 14, 2012).

*Svetlana Kunin*

As reported in the American Spectator: "China's Procurator officials went to the home of Deng Jiyuan to demand answers about how the photo was made available to the media, and to forbid them to speak to the media." (June 15, 2012).

Then in Yahoo! News: "The husband of a Chinese woman whose forced abortion seven months into her pregnancy caused an uproar has disappeared" (June 26, 2012).

Maria Conchita Alonso, Cuban actress, wrote an open letter critical of Sean Penn's praises of Hugo Chavez. Confident in his superior understanding of the world, Penn calls Alonso "a pig." She responds: "and you are a communist." I am afraid Penn may have taken it as a compliment.

What is it that people like Sean Penn, Thomas Freidman and five Supreme Court judges do not understand about freedom?

Chief Justice Roberts quoted Justice Holmes to explain his decision on ObamaCare: "Our plain duty is to adopt that which will save the act." He joined four judges, who call themselves liberal or progressive. These five justices help justify the power of the ever-growing government over individual American citizens. Victorious Nancy Pelosi, also from the liberal/progressive camp, tweeted: "Victory for the American people!"

In the USSR we lived under the slogan: "Everything belongs to the people!" In reality it meant that nothing belonged to the people, individual rights were limited and everything was controlled by the government, including media, the judiciary, and "free" services. Those who objected to the government power were "enemies of the people" and could end up in a gulag prisons. People who call themselves liberal or progressive like this model of government. As Friedman formulated, they admire a powerful government ruling over helpless citizens.

The liberal media faithfully defend all of President Obama's big government initiatives. Four Supreme Court judges are reliable rubber-stampers of any Obama policies. Gulags are not here yet, but National Public Radio is preoccupied with Romney donors, trying to obtain their names and personal information. Was Chief Justice Roberts afraid to be labeled the "enemy of the people"?

The Obama administration has put the country on the path of destruction of individual liberties, the dehumanizing power of bureaucrats and a substantial degradation of standards of living. Five Supreme Court Judges agreed with this direction. The transformation of the USA is well on its way.

Who cares how we will call this government-controlled society. In the 21$^{st}$ century, Obama doesn't need to confiscate private property to fully implement totalitarian control. The Affordable Care Act simply assumes control over our lives. Just as with the illusive goals of limiting "climate change" comes government control over air, land and seas.

The question is will we, the American people, be able to stop liberals and progressives? Or we will capitulate, as Chief Justice Roberts did, too scared to be branded by the left.

*President's Attack on Success Shows United States Falling, Not Rising*

Original publication date: July 24, 2012

In a speech on July 13 in Roanoke, Va., President Obama said this about successful people: "You didn't get there on your own. I'm always struck by people who think, well, it must be because I was just so smart. There are a lot of smart people out there. It must be because I worked harder than everybody else. Let me tell you something—there are a whole bunch of hard-working people out there. … If you were successful, somebody along the line gave you some help."

Why limit the discussion to the United States?

Everywhere on our planet, there are smart and hard-working people striving for success and a decent life. Like in the United States, every country has people building roads and using these roads to get to places of work; some people are good teachers, some are good farmers, etc. Most human societies have the same general components. I am sure Barack Obama saw plenty of smart and hard-working people in Indonesia, where he lived as a child. Why is Indonesia, a country very rich in natural resources, poor?

My husband, our friends and I worked hard in the USSR. Fresh from college, full of enthusiasm, we were in our prime years. Soviet communists had created a system according to teachings by Karl Marx. This system was based on the principles of equality: Rich exploiters (private business owners) didn't have a place in this "workers' paradise." Therefore, entrepreneurs were outlawed.

There were many talented inventors in the Soviet Union. To register their invention and obtain a patent, they had to include names of official communist leaders as co-creators, putting their names above their own. If government leaders could not comprehend the idea or its relevance to the future, the invention died. The same applied to works of art. In this "just society," people were whipped into conformity. Smart or not smart, all were equally poor.

Government central planners in the USSR, or China, or Cuba, didn't invent modern technology, and Soviet-made computers of the late 1970s were imitations of IBM's, created from stolen blueprints. Today, the modern Russian language is full of modified English terminology for all high-tech gadgets.

An Associated Press article dated June 4 and titled "Is Obama a Socialist?" stated: "In much of today's world, socialism lacks the contentious overtones that it has in America." Are they talking about Europe, where younger generations are realizing that their parents bankrupted their countries?

*Back in the USSR*

Original publication Date: August 22, 2012

'What exactly is the point of this article?" asked a reader of my last (July 25) column titled "President's Attack On Success Shows U.S. Falling, Not Rising." "That the U.S. has a robust private sector and a host of freedoms? That people with good ideas can succeed in America? Who is arguing these points?"

Too many people think that freedom, opportunity and a variety of choices are ever-present features of life in the U.S.—that fundamental transformation of America will not affect accustomed standards.

When we lived in the U.S.S.R., locked away from the world, kept from traveling abroad and surrounded by government-controlled sources of information, we couldn't imagine what kind of life people had on the outside. Simple things, like tomatoes in stores in winter, seemed improbable.

When we immigrated to the U.S., I realized that most of what we were taught about capitalism was false. I was surprised how uninformed and downright clueless Americans were regarding communist ideology and history. The platitudes of communist propaganda that were all around me in the Soviet Union were accepted as something new and wonderful by well-meaning people in the U.S. While Soviet citizens were excluded from the external world by their government, liberal/progressives in the "free world" were insulated from reality.

In the 1930s, when communists were starving the Russian people with regulations on farmers, New York Times correspondent Walter Duranty reported, "Any report of a famine in Russia is today an exaggeration or malignant propaganda." For his stories, Duranty won a Pulitzer Prize. Through the late 1950s, liberal newspapers in America ignored stories about work prison camps in the Soviet Union. But more than 20 million people accused of opposition to centralized government perished.

In 1956, Soviets brutally suppressed a revolt against the Soviet-imposed socialist government in Hungary. More than 2,500 Hungarians were killed. In 1968, Czechoslovakia lived through a similar uprising and suppression.

From late 1960s, Soviet dissidents raised their voices against the oppressive, inhumane rule of the communist government in the USSR. Dissidents were imprisoned, condemned to psychiatric facilities and expelled from work. Their families were persecuted.

Meantime, enjoying the freedoms of the U.S., Weather Underground radicals were calling forces to unite for "the destruction of U.S. imperialism and achieve ... world communism." By 1980, the centrally planned economy of the USSR was in shambles. By American standards the population lived below poverty level.

It's stunning for an immigrant from a socialist country to hear in the speeches of Democratic Party leaders platitudes taught in socialist countries. Even more stunning is how they resonate with people born in the free world.

At the end of 19th century and the beginning of 20th calls for "equality," "fairness," "sacrifices for collective good" and "social justice" aroused communist revolutionaries in Russia and ushered in the USSR. They demonized and obliterated any religion that interfered with government authority. They erased individualism and entrepreneurship from society. Animosity among ethnic groups was insidiously cultivated.

In the U.S., fascism and socialism are classified at the opposite ends of the political spectrum; in reality, these two ideologies have a lot in common.

Fascism is "a political philosophy, movement or regime that exalts nation and often race above the individual and that stands for a centralized autocratic government headed by a dictatorial leader, severe economic and social regimentation, and forcible suppression of opposition" (Merriam Webster's 11th Collegiate Dictionary).

That definition of fascism can easily be applied to the socialism I experienced. The only difference is that to organize communities of fateful followers, German fascists used an ideal of racial purity, and communists used class warfare. Fascists confiscated properties of non-Aryans, and communists confiscated all private properties.

Free market capitalism, which created a large, prosperous middle class in America, and government-centered ideologies have nothing in common. For more than 100 years, old and tired socialist propaganda brought out the worst in societies: envy, hate, intolerance and disrespect for human life, just as these traits have increased in the last four years in the U.S.

The U.S. is not 19$^{th}$ century tsarist Russia, but it is being transformed into something far different from the "land of the free." The softer-styled European welfare societies are falling apart, leaving future generations broke. Is there a chance Barack Obama's vision of centralized government, surrounded by a web of sclerotic bureaucracies, will create a fair society?

The same reader who commented on my July article continued: "Or is the grim description of life in the former Soviet Union meant to paint Obama and his party as communists/socialists/fellow travelers bent on destroying America and all it stands for?"

Yes, that's exactly what I mean—and Obama's rhetoric, actions and results confirm this point.

*Former Soviet Jews Ask: Why "Transform" the United States?*

Original publication date: September 20, 2012

My husband and I left the USSR in 1980. We were 30 years old and had no idea what was ahead. We were not looking for a paradise; we were running from the hell of a government-controlled society, where people are helpless against government power

The 2012 Democratic Party convention was a surreal sight for us: a parade of speakers, full of the arrogant assumption that others are not smart enough to accomplish anything without government guidance and intrusion. The Democratic candidate for U.S. Senate from Massachusetts, Elizabeth Warren, was one of these speakers. Almost a year before Barack Obama said, "If you've got a business, you didn't build that," Elizabeth Warren expounded on this same theme: "There is nobody in this country who got rich on his own—nobody," she said. "You built a factory out there? Good for you. But I want to be clear: "You moved your goods to market on the roads the rest of us paid for. You hired workers the rest of us paid to educate. You were safe in your factory because of police forces and fire forces that the rest of us paid for. You didn't have to worry that marauding bands would come and seize everything at your factory—and hire someone to protect against this—because of the work the rest of us did."

The inevitable conclusion from this statement is that what you think is yours, belongs to all people. The country needs government to "fairly" distribute what is everybody's. Behind this sophistry is an idea: that government can confiscate anything. We experienced the implementation of this type of thinking in the Soviet Union.

A younger speaker, Sandra Fluke, who is a year older than we were when we had the mission of finding liberty and emigrating from a socialist society, has a mission of free contraceptives for American women. Those who disagree with her mission are engaged in a "war on women."

Is Ms. Fluke's concern about free contraceptives really our concern? Do we have rights to our property, businesses, savings and income? Can the government prevent us from freely mentioning God in public places? Do we want a health care model where the

*Svetlana Kunin*

government gives us permission to seek out available treatment? Do we all belong to the government?

For many decades American progressives slowly weaved their ideas around this free society: political correctness, multiculturalism, religious intolerance and a rejection of the American value system. With the election of Barack Obama to the presidency of the USA in 2008, progressives reached the peak of their power.

The Occupy Wall Street movement—the pinnacle of progressive/liberal thought—filled the crowds with envy, malice toward hard work and hate toward accomplished people. Progressives of all stripes, from top Democratic Party leaders to Hollywood creatures such as Michael Moore, to old-guard America-haters like Professor Noam Chomsky and Bill Ayers, endorsed the Occupy movement. They hope that the envious malcontents will help them to finally finish off free-market capitalism.

The foreign policies of this Democratic Party administration do not provide solace either. In my Feb. 16, 2011, column I raised a question after witnessing in 2009 the inept Hilary Clinton passing her "Reset button" to the Russian foreign minister. Does this administration have the same "understanding" of reality when they insisted on "immediate" changes in Egypt, followed by similar events in Libya?

Today, with events in Egypt and the murder of the U.S. ambassador in Libya, in addition to the Russian submarine lurking undetected in the Gulf of Mexico, we have the answer to my question. Naiveté should end before your late 20s, and then, if you don't learn or comprehend the world around you, ignorance begins.

For many Jewish immigrants from socialist countries, one of the biggest disappointments is to see how many American Jews are actively supporting this modern Democratic Party, a party promoting powerful authoritarian government and dependent citizens. Jews had previously escaped from all kinds of Jew-hating authoritarian regimes: monarchies, fascists and communists. Like many other immigrants, they were poor when they came here but created a good life for their progeny. Today, their descendants are agitating for the transformation of America, trying to change the society that saved their grandparents into a society similar to those their ancestors escaped.

Facing humiliating anti-Semitism streaming down from a central government, we used to find consolation in the fact that, despite persecution, Jews are intelligent: they contribute to the world so many outstanding scientists, musicians, engineers, etc. But I question the intelligence of today's American Jews who, along with their liberal/progressive comrades, participate in the shredding of America's foundation. Do these people know any other country where minorities and poor immigrants can accomplish more than what these groups can achieve today in the USA?

Woody Allen's 1983 movie "Zelig" gives a plausible explanation of these progressive Jews' behavior. The main character, Leonard Zelig, has a pathological ability to mimic his surrounding idols. In order to find the cause of his strange behavior, psychiatrist hypnotized Zelig to reach his most inner thoughts.

In a deep, hypnotically induced sleep, Zelig finally revealed: "I want to be liked." The doctor wrote in her conclusion: "I myself felt that one could really think of him as the ultimate conformist."

*Svetlana Kunin*

The veracity of the caring-Jewish-mother stereotype will be tested on Nov. 6. Will they think about the future of their children, or are they more preoccupied with a desire to be liked by their progressive neighbors?

*In Democrats' America, We Follow the Government's Dreams*

Original publication date: November 5, 2012

Barack Obama pursued and achieved his own dream: He became the president of the United States of America. Today, the president's dream is to transform America into a country where citizens pursue dreams of the government.

Despite all evidence to the contrary, people believe in the propaganda about the goodness of centralized government. My husband and I were 30 years old when we immigrated in 1980. I have now lived half of my life in the government-controlled society of the USSR and the other half in the U.S. The president's rhetoric about fairness, equality, the collective good and promises of the government taking care of people is the same rhetoric I grew up with. Obama reiterates the same platitudes: He calls it moving America forward.

In the USSR, religion was almost eradicated from society about 20 years after the Russian Revolution. More recently, there was an attempt to remove references to God from the Democratic Party platform, as well as ongoing assaults on religious institutions inherent to Obama's health care regulations.

The most disturbing aspect of Obama's administration is its annoyance with freedom of speech, which is part of the ongoing subjugation of individual liberties to a government-defined common good. The devastating traits of an intrusive government, especially if the media, judges and government represent the same ideological unit, are a loss of individual freedom. The citizen is helpless in the face of bureaucratic authorities.

When, on Sept. 11, 2012, the American embassy was attacked in Egypt, followed by the murder of the ambassador and three other Americans in Libya, the administration, media and State Department attempted to concentrate public attention on an insignificant video clip as the reason for the attack. Strangely, the mainstream media, including NPR, at first speculated that the clip was produced by an Israeli Jew. Why, before any concrete information was available, was the ethnicity of the filmmaker so important to emphasize?

In a few days, the real religious identity of the author, a Coptic Christian, also was publicized. Was the pinpointing of his religion in this case more relevant than in the Fort Hood shooting, when the government/media/DOJ troika downplayed the terrorist's religion? In any case, the truth was this American citizen and his video had nothing to do with Benghazi.

In the case of the controversy surrounding the arrest of Harvard Professor Henry Louis Gates at his home in July 2009, both media and the presidential administration accused policeman of racial profiling. In the case of George Zimmerman, charged in the shooting of teenager Trayvon Martin in Florida, the media manipulated the audio tape, making a case of racism in America.

I don't see coordinated disinformation as just an accident. It's too reminiscent of what people regularly experience in totalitarian societies. There is something very unsettling about this administration's practice of classifying people by ethnicity, gender and economic status, rather than as Americans. There is something very dangerous when individuals are sacrificed for someone's idea of the common good.

I have first-hand experience of how powerful propaganda can be. Even when faced with the hardships of day-to-day life in the USSR, deficits, subpar medical care, corruption, political persecutions and the absence of freedoms, people continued to hope for a better future that communism promised. They believed that the capitalist alternative was much worse.

When we came to America, we found the freedom to pursue our dreams of an independent life. The cruel capitalist society, about which we were taught, did not exist in reality. In comparison, socialism seems inhumane and degrading, while capitalism provides opportunities and the decency inherent to an independent life.

Is it possible that by brainwashing others with anti-capitalist propaganda, progressives in this country brainwashed themselves to the point they are happy to entangle themselves and future generations in a web of soulless bureaucrats? Will demagoguery about rich vs. poor, black vs. whites, and hallucinations about losing access to free contraception and mass abortions result in the abortion of the American free enterprise system and individual liberties? Do we have enough freedom-loving voters to stop moving America backwards to where Europe was at the beginning of 20th century?

*Class- and Race-Conscious Society*

Original publication date: February 2, 2013

At the doctor's office this year I had to fill out newly required paperwork that included questions about my race and ethnicity. I chose the "refused to answer" option. I had been classified by ethnicity before in the Soviet Union, where every official document required indication of it. Our ethnicity, in turn, plus connections to the government, determined the level of our security and dignity. We found our dignity in the United States.

"We, the people, still believe that every citizen deserves a basic measure of security and dignity," President Obama declared in his second inaugural address. "We, the people, still believe that our obligations as Americans are not just to ourselves, but to all posterity."

We naturalized citizens take care of our families and children, and in addition to paying taxes we contribute to charities of our choice. What's wrong with that? By all classifications, we were poor immigrants in our first years in the USA. But we didn't feel poor in this land of abundance. Here, in the dynamic land of capitalism, there is an honest way out of poverty.

I find the classification of "poor" as degrading and discouraging. Old class-warfare demagoguery brought misery, poverty and hatred everywhere it was exercised.

"Being true to our founding documents," said Obama, "does not require us to agree on every contour of life; it does not mean we will all define liberty in exactly the same way, or follow the same precise path to happiness. Progress does not compel us to settle centuries-long debates about the role of government for all time but it does require us to act in our time."

The debate about the role of the government had a real-life test in the last century. Whether it was the National-Socialists of Germany and other fascist regimes, the liberal-socialism of Western Europe, or the communist dictatorships of the USSR, Eastern European countries, China, Cuba and North Korea all centralized regimes showed failing results, compared with the American experiment. The standard of living in the USA is higher for all, poor or rich.

As Soviet Communists did in the last century, the Obama administration is dividing citizens into groups, belittling the concept of individual liberties. At the same time, he glorifies the socialist ideal of a big, centralized government. Living in the comfortable world created by capitalist free enterprise, atrocity-deniers insist on a better world of a socialist utopia where they find equality and social justice.

Millions of talented people have perished as they refused to conform to equality; many who conformed sacrificed their talents to equate to mediocrity. Nobody knows how many Gershwins or Einsteins were cheated out of their dreams by government's ethnicity allocations. Because of his ethnicity, the father of Google co-founder Sergey Brin couldn't do what he wanted to do in the USSR, so he emigrated to the USA, where his son could pursue his dream.

How come we immigrants from socialist countries have found social justice here in the USA while native citizens have not? Ignorant of history and directed by capitalism-haters in schools, they have no idea how liberty and independence from a centralized state magnify the dimensions of life.

Old Soviet communists, who dreamed of and planted seeds for the demise of capitalism in the USA, now look upon the endless ignorance of Americans and rejoice. Modern America haters use this ignorance to finish the job.

*America's "Useful Idiots" Are Just Like Those in the USSR*

Original publication date: August 5, 2013

"We have overthrown capitalism," dictator Joseph Stalin declared in a February 1931 speech to the First All-Union Conference of Leading Personnel of Socialist Industry. "We have seized power. We have built up a mighty socialist industry. We have transferred the middle peasants on to the path of socialism. We have already accomplished what is most important from the point of view of construction. "Not much is left to do; to gain technique, to master science. And when this is achieved, our pace shall become such as we dare not even dream of at present."

Sixty years later, the world witnessed the collapse of one of the first socialist economies: that of the Soviet Union.

It's hard to believe that 100 years after the real-life test and failure of the Marxist theory of class warfare, collectivism and central planning, the American people are still buying into this tired ideology, with its superficial and primitive slogans.

Five years into the "we are all in this together" world of Barack Obama, low-income children continue to attend failing schools, bad teachers cannot be fired, jobs are disappearing, insurance premiums are rising, the IRS is oppressing opposition, the media repeat government talking points, government is snooping on citizens and investigating journalists, and the poor are stuck in poverty.

The United States is getting weaker on all fronts. The only power this administration is gaining is over the American citizens.

The tremendous efforts the Obama administration put into the Zimmerman trial to prove America is racist ended in fiasco. But citizens should not unwind with relief. Soviet Communists successfully practiced ethnic incitement to redirect disillusion and anger. Prejudices are present all over the world. But when government is involved in a business of incitement of racism and chauvinism, people are in mortal danger.

Living in the USSR for the first 30 years of my life, I have met many people who didn't believe that socialist government was responsible for their misery. The founder of the USSR, Vladimir Lenin, called such people "rotten intelligentsia."

In the USSR, I didn't quite understand this characterization. Only when I immigrated to the USA did I understand the difference between freedom and dictatorship. It can be characterized by one word: "dignity." When human beings are losing their ability to choose, they lose their dignity. The less choice they have, the more dignity they lose. Once frightened into submission and conformity, the "rotten intelligentsia" no longer represents any danger to the power of dictatorship.

Today in the U.S., I meet people who live in freedom and comfort but believe that the country should be transformed into a dictatorship of the government. Full of slavish admiration for power, brainwashed by Marxist propaganda and ignorant of history, some of them, such as commentator Thomas Freidman, admire the Chinese system of government.

Others, many of them from Hollywood, don't see any problems with the regimes in Cuba or Venezuela.

They demonize role models such as Clarence Thomas or Dr. Ben Carson, and glamorize Al Sharpton. They ignore independent thinkers such as Thomas Sowell, Walter Williams and other brilliant, accomplished individuals. Instead, they inflame racial grievances.

How ironic that the majority of Google employees, working for a company co-founded by the son of Soviet immigrants, support the transformation of free people into servants of the government. The company's chairman, Eric Schmidt, understood that Barack Obama needed more time to subordinate American people and was therefore very active in the president's re-election. I guess Mr. Schmidt liked what he saw in North Korea.

American liberals and progressives do not pose any danger to totalitarian government; they are eager to assist in its oppression. I must give Lenin credit for understanding the psychology of such people. Preoccupied with their personal image and status, indifferent to individual freedoms and void of any strong moral values, American progressives and liberals are the same people Lenin defined as "rotten intelligentsia."

Former card-carrying communists are the new Russian oligarchs. They can see through the Obama administration and the rest of American progressives. They were useful to Soviet Communists in the middle of last century; today, they are no longer useful.

Russians lived through all the slogans and actions of class warfare, fairness and equality. They were part of a centralized government and know too well how it works and how it ends.

*A Russian Immigrant Sees the United States*
*Making Same Mistakes as USSR*

Original publication date: September 5, 2013

Commenting on my column last month (Aug. 6), a reader lamented: "Authors writing about socialism need to know what socialism is. The author of this article would rather just go into a tirade about the problems in our country ... and automatically jump to the conclusion the problem is socialism. Huh? What? Where is the socialism you're talking about?"

An old Soviet joke goes as follows: "A Soviet and an America journalist argued about whose society is freer. The American declared, 'I can stand in front of the White House and yell that our president is a fool!' 'Big deal,' responded the Russian, 'I can stand in front of Kremlin in Moscow and yell that your president is a fool too!'"

This joke is at least 40 years old. But today in the U.S., very much as it was in the USSR, a rodeo clown's livelihood is in peril because he dared to make a joke about the president. One can measure level of socialism by the number of lives wasted, humiliated or destroyed by a centralized government that is pursuing its agenda and control.

Some people don't need to hit the wall to understand reality. Being brainwashed from childhood, I had to personally experience real life as an adult in the Soviet Union to have my illusions and naiveté about fairness shattered.

Living in a socialist country for 30 years of my life, and required to study the theory of Marxism/Leninism from elementary school through college,

I am familiar with some distinct characteristics of socialism. They include:

- Controlling people by making them dependent on government for basics such as medical care, property rights and income.
- Applying separate standards in medical and other services for government employees and acolytes vs. the rest of society.
- Brainwashing the population starting as early as possible with propaganda that is pro-central government and anti-free market capitalism.
- Polarizing society by dividing people into groups by ethnicity.
- Controlling speech, enforcing political correctness and attempting to suppress opposition media.
- Collecting citizens' personal information using all resources available, including NSA programs.
- Intimidating opposition through Justice Department investigations of journalists, IRS intimidation of groups and individuals who oppose government policies, and information collected on citizens that becomes quite handy.
- Demonizing and destroying the livelihood of anyone—from members of the Tea Party to rodeo clowns—who dares to criticize the president.
- Controlling economic resources via EPA and other regulations despite negative economic consequences.

*Svetlana Kunin*

- Conducting show trials of freethinkers, such as the 13 felony counts brought against Internet prodigy Aaron Swartz, potentially leading to 30 years imprisonment.
- Calling for sacrifices in the name of the collective good, promises of a bright future and endless lies about disastrous government failures here and now.

A prominent Soviet physicist, Lev Landau, defined the USSR's system as "a dictatorship of bureaucrats." It amounted to socialism, he said, "because the means of production do not belong to the people, but to bureaucrats."

Landau was arrested in USSR in April 1938 for criticizing the government. He was released a year later because Stalin needed his genius to work on Soviet atomic and hydrogen bombs. He couldn't accept the 1962 Nobel Prize for physics in person after the car he was driving that January was hit by an oncoming truck.

When our family emigrated from the USSR to America, leaving our relatives and friends behind, a house and car weren't part of our American Dream. I don't think people risking their lives today, floating in small boats from Cuba to America, for instance, have houses and cars in mind.

We wanted to be free from the permission needed from government bureaucrats at every step of our lives, from government instigation of religious intolerance and from ethnic quotas at places of learning and work.

My American dream was realized on the first day we stepped onto the American soil, with two suitcases and $300. What's the dream of those who vote for the party of centralized government, government bureaucracies and idolized leaders?

## By Weakening America, Obama Plays into Putin's Hands

Original publication date: September 25, 2013

Vladimir Putin chose the New York Times to publish his op-ed questioning American exceptionalism. No surprise there: For almost a century, the Times has exhibited sympathy toward good old communists, and has always been eager to publish their propaganda.

The question is why would the Russian president, a former KGB communist and present Russian oligarch, write this op-ed? Is it to show the American people that Obama's administration has disastrous standing in the Middle East?

I don't think so. The dream of American demise didn't expire with the collapse of the USSR, and the dream of Russian superiority and influence in the world didn't leave the minds of Russian nationalists. By transforming America, the Obama administration, with the support of progressive journalists, college professors, liberal judges and pop-culture moguls, is actively participating in the realization of Russia's dreams.

In his new book "On Constitutional Disobedience," Professor Louis Michael Seidman of the Georgetown University Law Center asks why we should care about what the constitution says, and how we can make decisions today based on a document created more than 200 years ago.

In September 2011, Elizabeth Warren, former professor at the Harvard Law School and now

U.S. senator from Massachusetts, declared: "There is nobody in this country who got rich on his own—nobody."

Professor Grover Furr of Montclair State University insisted that Stalin didn't commit any crimes and that "the history of the Soviet Union is the most falsified."

American progressives are with Putin. Why then, did he write his op-ed?

After lecturing about politics in the Middle East, Putin objected to President Obama's mention of U.S. exceptionalism. "With modest effort and risk," Obama said, "we can stop children from being gassed and thereby make our own children safer over the long run. I believe we should act. That's what makes America different. That's what makes us exceptional."

The Russian president reminded us in his op-ed that "God created us equal," but he didn't clarify that centralized government can, and always does, determine who is "more equal than others." American progressives in government and their acolytes already know that.

I believe the intended target of Putin's op-ed were Americans who still believe, as I do, in the uniqueness of this country.

Professor Robert Gordon at Northwestern University contends the Industrial Revolution was a random accident, and that the continuum of progress and prosperity in the U.S. is over. But Gordon's theory is refuted by immigrants' stories. We came from countries where centralized dogmas and dictates from government leaders overrode citizens own thinking and creative abilities.

There were roads, bridges, schools, police and an army in the former Soviet Union; religious symbols were eliminated from the public space and equality was achieved by making everybody poor.

Vaclav Havel, a dissident playwright who in 1989 became the hero of Czechoslovakia's "Velvet Revolution," and then became the first democratically elected president of the Czech Republic, said: "Out of gifted and sovereign people, the regime made us little screws in a monstrously big, rattling and stinking machine."

Real stories of endless immigrants to the United States are a good illustration of how ordinary people, released from oppressive societies, contributed to its progress, and many achieved extraordinary results. America is an exceptional country because the centerpieces of its founding system are individual liberty and guaranteed rights. Free people, pursuing their dreams without government intrusion, created a prosperous and technologically advanced society.

Professors Seidman, Furr and Gordon, Sen. Warren, the Obama administration and the rest of their progressive kin do not understand what made exceptional progress and prosperity in America possible.

President Putin knows that American progressives are working on the demise of this country. He is trying to brainwash those who still believe in America and its constitution. The confirmation is that while the shooting at the Navy Yard in Washington, D.C., was still in progress, the chairman of the foreign affairs of Russia's Parliament, Alexei Pushkov, tweeted: "The USA should part with the notion of American exceptionalism. It contradicts the principles of equal rights and smells of political racism."

Russians know which keywords to use to make American progressives kick.

I hope American patriots will not be fooled.

*Soviet Dissidents Miraculously Won a Hopeless Fight*

Original publication date: October 29, 2013

Nikolai Ezhov, chief of the Soviet secret police (NKVD, later KGB) under Joseph Stalin in the 1930s, once provided the best definition of socialist government: "There is nothing to be afraid of now," he said. "All power is in our hands. We execute whom we want and absolve whom we want."

When Soviet dissidents in the '60s and '70s dared to voice objections against government tyranny, they were demonized, humiliated and fired from their jobs. Many were forced into prison and psychiatric facilities, powerless against government judges, bureaucrats and media.

Forty years after the Russian Revolution, the majority of the Soviet people never lived in a free society. Many were sympathetic to the dissidents' cause but too afraid to openly express their support. Others were so brainwashed they were happy with the dissidents' persecutions.

Nobody, however, had to ask what the dissidents' endgame was. Supporters or not, they understood dissidents were screaming for human rights and freedom. Their fight seemed hopeless. But, miraculously, the dissidents won. Western human-rights activists smuggled dissidents' stories out from behind the Iron Curtain and exposed the cruel nature of the communists. Soviets were forced to let dissidents leave the country. Because of these brave souls' cry for freedom, many Soviet Jews, including me, were able to escape from Russian chauvinism, social quotas and oppression.

When dissidents mounted their fight for freedom in the Soviet Union, well-fed punks, such as Bill Ayers, co-founder of the Weather Underground in the '60s and now an education theorist, were agitating for socialism in America.

At the time refugees from the Soviet Union, Cuba, China, Czechoslovakia and Poland found freedom in the USA, American academics promoted socialism among their clueless students.

Today, admirers of centralized government have the power. The modern Democratic Party is a party of socialist/social-engineers and militant bureaucrats. They are treating citizens like herds of people—units void of individualism. As good old communists in the Soviet Union, Democrats insert government bureaucrats into every area of people's life—between parents and school choice for their kids, between teachers and children, between patients and doctors, between the ill and life-saving procedures and medications, and between inventors and their ability to implement their inventions.

They distort the family's role in nurturing and bringing up children. They control private enterprise through grants and regulations. They seek control over people through programs like ObamaCare.

Republicans who hurriedly criticize Sens. Ted Cruz and Mike Lee who resist such encroachments need to explain: What was the strategy and the endgame of Republicans who, during the George W. Bush administration, allowed a barrage of misleading accusations to go unanswered? Did they succeed against Democrat propaganda and misinformation?

In 2010 President Obama nominated Elena Kagan, who as Harvard Law School dean removed the U.S. constitutional law from the list of required subjects.

What was the strategy of Republican senators who joined Democrats and voted for her nomination to Supreme Court? Did they expect that at the end she would put the Constitution above her ideology?

During the Clinton presidency, Eric Holder obtained pardon for members of a Puerto Rican terror group; his law firm worked pro bono for Islamic terrorists. What was the strategy and endgame of Republicans who joined Democrats and approved Eric Holder to be U.S. attorney general? Whom did they expect Mr. Holder to protect: common folks or the likes of Black Panthers, who in 2008 intimidated people at polling places?

Why weren't Republicans alarmed from 2010 through 2013, while the IRS humiliated Tea Party groups and stalled their applications for tax-exempt status? What was the endgame of the last two feeble Republican presidential campaigns?

President Obama is about to destroy the freedom of the American people to make their own choices in life. His transformation of America will affect all races, genders, sexual orientations and classes. Political dancing around the corners, political correctness and archaic collegiality cannot push back a growing web of government bureaucrats. Soviet dissidents were facing life-threatening reprisals from the government. What are Republicans afraid of?

Ronald Reagan said: "Evil is powerless if the good are unafraid."

Only courageous, eloquent leaders and unabashed proponents of individual liberties can expose the inhumane nature of a socialist construct veiled by demagoguery about fairness and equality. Only exposure can save individual aspirations and progress. That's why I cheer Ted Cruz, Mike Lee and everyone who stands with them.

*America's Spoiled Left Is Clueless About Ukraine's Revolt*

Original publication date: March 5, 2014

In 1918, the Russian poet Alexander Blok, born into a sophisticated intellectual family, inspired by revolutionary calls for "equality," "fairness" and "social justice," wrote the poems "Twelve" and "The Scythians," glorifying the Russian socialist revolution. The same year he wrote an essay, "Intelligentsia and Revolution," in support of a new central communist government. Two years later, disillusioned, he complained to his friends that he had lost "faith in the wisdom of humanity." In 1921, Blok pleaded for the "freedom of creation."

By 1937, covert moles, imbedded in places of work and media, reported any form of insubordination to the Soviet government. About 5 million dutiful Soviet citizens sent denunciations about their neighbors' anti-government leanings. As a result, innocent human beings were sent to labor camps (gulags).

By the end of the 1980s, Soviets descended into poverty, alcoholism and hopelessness. The grand finale—the economic collapse of the USSR, the first socialist country—came in 1991.

Historical events didn't teach American progressives anything. They think that what happened in the Soviet Union doesn't have any correlation to their "noble" aspirations for government doing "good" on behalf of the people.

I look at spoiled brats such as professor of education Bill Ayers. They are very brave about criticizing free democracies like the U.S. or Israel, while living in a free democracy.

Did they ever try to criticize totalitarian regimes while residing within their dominion?

Or the strange case of Angela Davis, professor of history of consciousness at the University of California, Santa Cruz. Anyone who lived in the 1970s in the USSR remembers her name. "Freedom to Angela Davis" was on front pages of newspapers around the Soviet Union. The Soviet government awarded her with a Lenin Jubilee Medal for "valorous work (for military valor)" in 1972. The same year she received the National Order of the "Bay of Pigs" from Cuba's government.

In 1979, the Soviet government presented her with the International Lenin Prize (originally the International Stalin Prize) "for peace between peoples." Soviet communists murdered more than 20 million Soviet citizens. What kind of consciousness did Professor Davis teach?

Today in the United States of America:

- People are afraid to reveal their conservative values because they may lose their job.
- The Justice Department investigates and intimidates activists critical of the president.
- The media and IRS demonize groups and citizens opposing Democratic Party policies.
- The FCC wanted to dispatch "researchers" to newsrooms across America to demand "voluntary" compliance with how news stories are decided.

- Century-old slogans about "equality," "fairness," "common good" and "social justice" are centerpieces of Democratic Party policies.

In the 1960s, we learned in Soviet schools that the superior system of communism will spread and replace rotten capitalism. We were taught, however, that capitalist exploiters will not willfully give up their grip on the poor proletariat. Therefore, good and righteous communists must help.

In 1958, American author and ex-FBI agent Cleon Skousen wrote "The Naked Communist," a book listing 45 communist strategies for toppling capitalism from the inside. Some American scholars, like Professor Jack Rakove of Stanford University, accused him of "inventing fantastic ideas."

Half a century later, many items from this list eerily reflect modern Democratic Party postulates and strategies:

**No. 3:** Develop the illusion that total disarmament by the U.S. would be a demonstration of moral strength.

**No. 25:** Break down cultural standards of morality by promoting pornography and obscenity in books, magazines, motion pictures, radio and TV.

**No. 28:** Eliminate prayer or any religious expression in the schools on the grounds that it violates the principle of "separation of church and state."

**No. 29:** Discredit the American Constitution by calling it inadequate, old-fashioned, out of step with modern needs, a hindrance to cooperation between nations on a worldwide basis.

**No. 30:** Discredit America's Founding Fathers. Present them as selfish aristocrats who had no concern for the "common man."

**No. 31:** Belittle all forms of American culture and discourage the teaching of American history on the grounds it was only a minor part of the "big picture."

**No. 40:** Discredit the family as an institution. Encourage promiscuity and easy divorce.

**No. 41:** Emphasize the need to raise children away from the negative influence of parents. Attribute prejudices, mental blocks and the retarding of children's abilities to suppressive influence of parents.

It seems the U.S. is fatefully marching according to the plan designed by people long gone and rebuked by history. In fact, Soviet-era jokes translate perfectly to the United States of today:

- People who don't succeed in life—demand to forbid, confiscate and redistribute! (Mikhail Zhvanetsky, Russian satirist)
- If a federal organization is not corrupt— nobody needs it. (Leonid Shebarshin, former head of the foreign intelligence service of the KGB USSR)
- Government works very well; people are miserable because they don't work in the government. (Soviet joke)
- Central government guarantees that all people earn a "sustainable leaving minimum": that is a scientific calculation of people's needs that allows government rulers to have a good life. (Soviet joke)

Feeding off the riches made possible by free-market capitalism, Democrats throw out the dignity of self-reliance in favor of the inhumane ideals of government-enforced equality, quotas and limited choices.

Supporters of these policies don't have a clue why people are protesting today on the streets of Ukraine and Venezuela.

*Svetlana Kunin*

# Conclusion

When the Russian Revolution took place in 1917, the new Socialist ideals were fresh and appealing. Revolutionaries included believers of all stripes—from peasants to aristocrats. Young Jews from the Pale of Settlement, including my parents, were among the believers. However, the promises made did not materialize. The destruction of the old order was followed by top down control, disillusion, apathy and a low standard of living. God-based religion was eliminated from the public sphere. Churches and synagogues were demolished or converted to other uses. Private property was confiscated, business owners were vilified, and the government regulated every aspect of peoples' lives in the name of the greater good. To redirect populous anger, the Soviet government stirred up ethnical animosity, especially anti-Semitism.

For the last fifteen years, I have observed the transformation of the American Democratic Party. This party's aspiration of centralized control over civil society is very similar to any Communist party aspirations of past or present. Knowingly or not, Democrats reinstate Communists' tools of agitation: class warfare slogans, dividing citizens into group and pinning one group against another, fighting against religious believers, and imposing control over private ownership.

The most piercing trait of centralized government is control over mass media. "The press should be not only a collective propagandist and a collective agitator, but also a collective organizer of the masses," wrote Vladimir Lenin, leader of the first Communist government in Russia. He continued: "He who now talks about the freedom of the press goes backward and halts our headlong course toward socialism."

Today's American media obediently follow that direction. In one voice they recite Democratic Party talking points, while of social media rulers dutifully censor conservative postings. What a disgrace.

In 1961 Russian-born artist and writer Yury Pavlovich Annenkov (1889–1974) published a memoir, in which he refers to Lenin's note from 1924: "The capitalists of the whole world and their governments in pursuit of the Soviet market ... will open loans that will serve us ... and supply us with materials and techniques we are lacking. They will restore our military. In other words they will work on preparing their own suicide!"

The Soviet market is no more, but this prophetic quote is very relevant today. Multitudes of American companies are happily investing into the Communist Chinese economy. Many companies, like Google, would rather help Chinese Communist leaders than the American Department of Defense. It's hard to believe that any person would voluntarily give up guaranteed liberties in exchange for life under government directives and bounds. But brainwashed from many sides, American liberals are following the trajectory set for them a hundred years ago.

I remember my father's eyes when in 1980 our train was leaving from train station in Minsk, USSR. He didn't expect to see us again but hoped that we would be free to pursue a better life. Today people in Honk Kong are screaming for freedom from Communists. Will American people retain theirs?

Printed in the United States
By Bookmasters